THE DREAM THEATER
Keyboard Experience
Featuring Jordan Rudess

KEYBOARD TRANSCRIPTIONS • VOCAL

CONTENTS

Interview with Jordan Rudess 2
Lead Notation Guide 14

Keyboard Exercises by Jordan Rudess

Pitch Bending *(Bending Time)* 14
Arpeggiated Chord Inversions *(Spacetude Vest)* 32
Repeated Figures with Shifting Accent Patterns *(Dancing Home)* 46
Two-Handed Playing of Wide-Range Melodic Leads *(Hand Faith)* 66
Synchronization Between Left and Right Hands Playing Parallel Figures *(Honor Your Teacher)* 86
Alternation Between Triplet and Sixteenth-Note Rhythms in Lead Lines *(Octawizard)* 107
Extremely Rapid Passages *(Bee Enemy)* 146
Polyphonic Lead Playing *(The Lost Etude)* 189

Dream Theater Keyboard Transcriptions

Song	Album	Page
Take the Time	Images and Words	16
Space-Dye Vest	Awake	34
Scene Six: Home	Metropolis, Part 2: Scenes from a Memory	48
Blind Faith	Six Degrees of Inner Turbulence	68
Honor Thy Father	Train of Thought	88
Octavarium	Octavarium	110
In the Presence of Enemies - Part 1	Systematic Chaos	148
The Ministry of Lost Souls	Systematic Chaos	192
In the Presence of Enemies - Part 2	Systematic Chaos	164

Alfred Publishing Co., Inc.
16320 Roscoe Blvd., Suite 100
P.O. Box 10003
Van Nuys, CA 91410-0003
alfred.com

Copyright © MMIX by Alfred Publishing Co., Inc.
All rights reserved. Printed in USA.

ISBN-10: 0-7390-5801-0
ISBN-13: 978-0-7390-5801-5

Music transcribed and engraved by Chris Romero, except "Take the Time," transcribed and engraved by Jordan Baker

Front cover photography and layout © 2008 Paul Undersinger
Back cover photography © Janet Balmer
Interior cover photography © Janet Balmer, except Continuum fingerboard photo © Atsushi Sato

Jordan speaks!
In this exclusive interview conducted by his longtime music transcriber Chris Romero, Jordan Rudess invites us to join him for a discussion about his ongoing musical journey.

Photo © Atsushi Sato

How did you get your start in music?

I started playing music when I was seven years old. In second grade, there was a small upright piano in the corner of the classroom, and most days I would make my way over to the upright to play and accompany the kids in the various songs they would sing. It was all a lot of fun, and one day my teacher was talking to my mother and said, "Jordan plays the piano so well. It's so nice to have him playing all the time in class." My mother responded, "What are you talking about? We don't even own a piano. We've never seen him play," and the teacher said, "Well you'd better buy one because he's really talented." It wasn't more than a week before a small white baby grand Estey showed up at my house, and I started taking music lessons.

My first teacher was someone who noticed that I had a certain level of talent, so he quickly abandoned his usual teaching method and instead began to show me all the chords on the piano. I remember he would write out chord symbols like "C," "G," and "Gm," and I quickly learned how to improvise over those chords. In my early years, I also remember my mother bringing home guitar music that had only the melody written with a chord symbol over it. Without thinking about it, I would play my own arrangements of the songs.

When my parents realized where I was musically, they decided I needed a new teacher. My mother found a Hungarian woman, named Magda Steeg, who lived in Queens, New York, and she was a very serious teacher. I studied with Magda for a year and she prepared me for Julliard. The funny thing was that Magda's son, Bruce Steeg, was a Julliard-trained pianist who veered off that path to play in Guy Lombardo's band. So when Magda found me, she was excited because I would be the one to stay on course and be a classical pianist. Of course, things didn't end up that way!

I went to Julliard and stayed there through the preparatory division. By the time I got around college age, I started getting interested in other forms of music, including progressive rock. I started listening to bands like Genesis, Gentle Giant, and Yes, and these bands provided food for my imagination and made me feel like I wanted to explore some new avenues in music. One day, a few kids showed up at my house holding a Moog Sonic V synthesizer. We went to my bedroom, put on headphones, started playing, and the rest is history because that moment really changed my whole way of thinking about keyboards. I stayed at Julliard for a year or so at the college level and then decided to go off and explore my own music and technology.

What did you want to accomplish in the synthesizer world?

At first, I didn't really have a career path in mind. I was always focused on the artistic element of what I was doing and the way the synthesizers made me feel. I became fascinated with exploring different tones and learning about the control that I could have over the synthesizer. I was especially fascinated with pitch bending. Coming from a world where pitches were basically static, I found that I could have the freedom of other instrumentalists who could bend pitch. One of my first goals after I discovered this new technology was to be able to develop full control over my pitch bending technique. I would create exercises to help me practice bending, and I would also listen to other keyboardists. The first player who really blew my mind with his pitch bending technique was Patrick Moraz. In the song, "Someday" off the *Refugee* album, Patrick played a soaring lead with his Minimoog. The instant I heard this lead, I knew I needed my own Minimoog. I was also influenced by George Duke and Jan Hammer.

My first instrument that I owned was a Minimoog. I remember learning what each and every knob did and what different combinations of various knobs did to the sound. Looking back, I realize I didn't know any of the technical terms for what the knobs were doing to the sound, but I still knew how to create any sound that I wanted. It wasn't until later, when I worked at Korg and Kurzweil, that I learned the labels for all of the technical aspects of synthesizers, such as LFOs, sine waves, sawtooth waves, attack, decay, sustain, release, etc. Nowadays, people can go to universities to study synthesis, but when I was growing up there wasn't a lot of information readily available. Also, since I came from a Julliard background, I had to rebel and go off to learn it myself. My education came from being in the field, working with various synthesizer companies, and teaching concepts to other people. Even though I am much more of a musical person than a technical person, my love for the sounds that synthesizers can create always motivates me to spend the time it takes to learn the technical aspects of creating the sounds I want.

What projects or bands were you involved with before joining Dream Theater?

After I left Julliard, I was not very focused on a set career path. I ended up in the small ensemble Complex, where I played Minimoog with Sal Gallina, who was instrumental in inventing the WX7 wind controller, and Joseph Lyons who played an experimental instrument called the Cromulizer. Lyons invented this instrument, which used a Plexiglass tube and a bunch of elevator switches on it that were set up in a fingering similar to a bassoon. We would go around playing space music at universities on midnight radio shows. I still do stuff like this to this day. Just recently, I jammed with my neighbor, Richard Lainhart, who also experiments with space music and various forms of synthesis. We got together and did a live Internet broadcast, and I brought my Minimoog over.

Somewhere along the way, I got a call from a group called Speedway Boulevard. I had just met a girl and was living in Maryland at the time. I was supporting myself by playing cocktail music at nice hotels and restaurants. I never had much money and didn't own any synthesizers, but I was always able to support myself since I could always show up somewhere to play some tunes. When I got the call from SB, they were living in the studio while recording and called me to replace their current keyboardist, who was about to leave. They had found me through some people who worked at a studio where I recorded a demo much earlier around when I was sixteen, and those people remembered me and recommended me to SB. I was very excited. I lived in the studio for about a year, and I remember while tracking the music thinking that we were going to be the most famous band ever. We finished the project, and the record came out. It was quickly dropped by the record company.

At one point, I joined a tri-state band, which was well known in the area but more oriented towards playing at various high school functions and local clubs. The band was Apricot Brandy. Eventually, I moved to NYC because an old friend of mine started up a company and was doing some work with computers and music and graphics. I then became a project specialist for Korg, and this was the first time that I really started to think about how to take my talent and make a career out of it. Korg gave me the opportunity to travel around, meet people, and play at the NAMM and AES shows. Around this time, *Keyboard* magazine became interested in what I was doing.

Somewhere along this line, I got a call from Jan Hammer. He had met me at a NAMM show, and he wanted me to join him and legendary drummer Tony Williams to tour with their music. At the time, I had no idea who Tony Williams was, because I was not as familiar with jazz or even Miles Davis. Later, I realized just how famous he was, and suddenly it made sense why everyone would chant, "Tony, Tony, Tony!" at all the shows.

Later, I worked with guitarist Vinnie Moore on his album called *Time Odyssey*. I met Vinnie while working as a musical director for my friend's company. I showed up at one of the conventions with a small, portable, battery-operated Yamaha keyboard, called the CS01. I was walking along the halls and I saw Vinnie playing and asked if I could jam with him, and we did. Later on, when Vinnie was about to record his album, he remembered us jamming and wanted to find me to play on the album. His manager spent several months tracking me down before I was finally contacted.

I started to focus more on solo albums after that, and I recorded my first solo album, *Listen*. I left Korg and moved to Arizona to make the album. It was a big step for me, because I was finally able to create new music that mixed the various styles floating around in my head. At some point, I realized I needed to make money again, though.

Along the way, I met Chris Martirano from Kurzweil, who had extended an open invitation to me to work with them. I got a job as a product specialist, and soon after, my career began to speed up. I got calls from both The Dregs and Dream Theater at around the same time. I was debating which group to work with, and after some therapy with Steve Morse of The Dregs, I decided to join them. Working with The Dregs later led to the formation of my power duo group, the Rudess/Morgenstein Project, with Rod Morgenstein on drums.

The original Dream Theater call came in 1994, around the time when Kevin Moore was leaving the band. They had finished the *Awake* album and were about to tour. They needed someone to fill in at an important gig called the Foundations Forum. They also needed someone to join the group as a permanent member. I decided to play the Forum gig but then joined The Dregs instead. Sometime after, I got a call from Magna Carta records saying that Mike Portnoy was interested in putting together a "supergroup" of some of the best musicians on their instruments. I thought it was a cool idea and would give me a chance to play with some great musicians. Thus, Liquid Tension Experiment was born. We ended up doing two very successful instrumental albums with LTE. After those albums, Mike asked me again if I would join DT. The circumstances had changed a lot in a few years, and after thinking about it, I decided to join. The first album I worked on with them was *Metropolis Part 2: Scenes from a Memory*.

What is the writing process like in Dream Theater? How do you go about choosing sounds?

When I joined the group, I was told the group likes to be together for the writing process. When I prepared for the *Scenes* recording, I remember writing down all sorts of riffs, sequences, and ideas beforehand. I did all this preliminary work, but soon realized that not all of my ideas would necessarily fit within the Dream Theater mold. While DT's style is very broad and mixes elements from various genres, there are still a set of parameters that make each song a Dream Theater song. Mike Portnoy and John Petrucci were there from the beginning of Dream Theater, and they always have a clear vision of what they want to create. I was invited because of my extensive background, not just with classical music, but also with synthesizers. I brought some new compositional energy and also provided a musical partner who could keep up with, and inspire, John. So I had to learn to balance bringing a lot of new ideas to the table while also being able to understand that not all of these ideas would work within the Dream Theater vision. I developed a routine of generally starting with less ideas at the beginning of the writing process.

We start with a lot of writing in the same room together. A typical session will begin with John playing a riff, and then I'll suddenly get inspired by that riff. Or perhaps I have two chords that start a progression, and then John or Mike will say, "Oh, what if we go to this chord after that," or they will figure out how to work it into an entire section. Inspiration builds off inspiration. We always joke that there is no shortage of riffs in DT. Rather, the challenge lies in organizing and managing the ideas we have come up with. Mike is really great at forming a "Dream Theater arrangement" of the ideas that John and I have developed while riffing off each other. The rough arrangement is funny to think about because it usually ends up sounding like, "alright, we'll go to that verse, then we'll go to the B section, then we'll go to the bridge, then we'll go back to the verse, the B section, the chorus, then we'll repeat the verse, do the bridge three times…" At this point I'm usually laughing because I can't mentally follow where the song will go, and I don't know yet without hearing the arrangement how it will sound, but Mike always has a clear idea about the bigger picture. We write quickly. Even the longest songs take at most four days to put together conceptually before we are ready to begin recording, and a shorter song will be written in just one to two days.

One of the challenges of joining a group like Dream Theater, which has a lot of metal in the sound, is that many of the keyboard sounds in existence are really wimpy by comparison to the heaviness of the drums, bass, and guitars. Often, the stock lead patches on any keyboard will sound weak and not cut through. The kind of sounds I need to play along and be part of the band are aggressive, heavy sounds that you don't normally find in stock program banks. I started to slowly, but surely, create my own "cool" sounds as we recorded new albums. Because of all this previous work of developing sounds, I now have a whole library of sounds at my disposal that work with the other heavier sounds of the band. Some of these patches you will see in this book, like the "Snarling Pig," which has become a DT favorite. Now that the band has become accustomed to some of my sounds, we will sometimes write a section and everyone knows right away that we should use a particular sound that I created. "Use the pig sound!" However, even with this whole collection of roughly 1,000 sounds, there is still a need to create new patches. Oftentimes, it turns out I want all kinds of new things to happen with a particular patch, and so I have to program a new sound to make it happen.

Your lead playing is a signature mark of your style. What special techniques do you use for lead playing?

Lead playing is a technique I've developed over the years. It is difficult to form a consistent technique in some cases, because every keyboard has a different approach to pitch bending or other related techniques. Some keyboards have pitch wheels and mod wheels, some use a joystick, and some have extra switches that can be programmed. Also, I am constantly upgrading my setup to keep up with technology changes and improvements. This means that I am constantly reinventing my lead sound and my approach to how I create this sound. One thing that I do keep consistent is my pitch bend range. I like to have the upward pitch bend cover a whole step, while the downward pitch bend goes an entire octave. It gives me the flexibility to do various inflections. I can do dive bomb types of sounds, but I can also rise up into the pitch by bringing my pitch wheel down before I play the note. A lot of these effects emulate what a guitar player might perform with a whammy bar.

My lead sounds change a little bit, though, over time. When I used to play the Kurzweil K2500/2600, there were some unique parameters I had on one of my lead sounds. I had this really cool sound that I made with the help of Chris Martirano at Kurzweil. We were sending our different versions of this lead back and forth through emails as we perfected it. The lead started with the basic JR tone, but it used the two switches above the pitch wheel and mod wheel. Those two switches did some cool stuff. We used function generators to create a lag (a different lag with each button), and each time you hit a switch, it would, over time, get rid of the fundamental tone and slowly bring in a feedback tone. Each switch brought in a different feedback tone. As you brought the mod wheel up, it would cycle through and blend various harmonics. The sliders on the Kurzweil also brought in other harmonics. This lead sound ended up being my most involved sound, and you can hear a great example of it in my solo in "Honor Thy Father."

On the Korg Oasys, my current keyboard, I worked with Peter Schwartz to port my lead sound over. He had been programming the Oasys for Korg as it was being released, and so he had a lot of in-depth knowledge with the instrument. Peter helped me get the original tone that I wanted back, although I had to adapt to using the left-right movement of the joystick instead of the up-down movement of the pitch wheel for bending. When you push the joystick up, my Oasys lead patch gets rid of the fundamental and brings in a harmonic. You can get the same effect by pulling the joystick down toward you, but it produces a different harmonic. There are also two switches that can further alter which feedback tone gets brought in with the joystick. There is also a small ribbon controller, which we programmed to bring in a nastier distortion to my lead sound.

I've also ported my lead sound to the Roland Fantom. On the Fantom, the joystick only goes one way, so my lead sound is a bit simpler and the sound itself is also cleaner. This lead sound is more of a pure sound, comparable to my older JR lead that you can hear in a song like "Fatal Tragedy." Now, I have so many lead sounds, that often I will mix them while we record a new album.

What advice do you have for players looking to improve their technique, improvisation, composition, and preparation for recording and live settings?

What is interesting about entering the synthesizer world is that you are always traveling on new ground. I was starting to deal more with computers and sounds that were electronically generated. Other processes like quantization or speeding things up were also at my disposal. Keyboardists somehow have to work in a world where the technology can also manipulate your sound and do pretty much anything you want it to. With computers, you can get things to sound so even and controlled. This has inspired me to work with sounds where you need to constantly move your fingers to keep the sound going.

The world of technology definitely influences one's physicality in how one interacts with and produces music. Technology can inspire people to practice new and different things. I think of playing keyboards like a physical sport. You need to have the patience to develop the motor skills and muscles in your fingers and flexibility to be able to play. You might have some great ideas in your head, but when you sit down to play, the ideas can stop because you can't get them out physically. One of the things that helps you get past this problem is training your fingers to move. Then you need to be able to know where to move them to, and this involves developing your ear. I recommend singing along with a keyboard. I'll often take a simple bass line and loop it in the left hand, and while I'm playing this line, I'll start improvising in the right hand and I'll sing the melody while I'm playing it. This is a key technique to practice because it forces you to connect your inner voice with your outer physicality, which allows you to play what you hear in your head.

Let's say you want to learn the blues. To do this, you need to start by learning how to play the blues scale in every key. What if the guitarist says, "Let's do a blues in B-flat?" Maybe you can hear it in your mind, but you'll have a harder time getting your fingers to naturally be in the right place on the keyboard. If you practice all the scales, though, and you have all of these scales and arpeggios in your fingers, then you'll have an easier time. You want to create a library of riffs and patterns that is inside of your fingers that you can pull out quickly. Over the years, I've discovered lots of riffs and arpeggios that I've liked; some are traditional, but others might be variations or modal based. When I was first learning chords and inversions, I would start by playing a C chord (or pick a chord), and then I would immediately find every inversion of that chord. After practicing this method enough, you get to the point where you don't even have to think about it. One day when I was young, I heard another pianist who was playing jazzy chords like dominant sharp-9 chords. I was immediately struck by the sound of the chord, so when I got home, I sat at the piano and started to find all the dominant sharp-9 chords in every possible position. This led me to look for all the various 13 chords, and then I later created an exercise that worked these two types of chords together.

Another pivotal point in my learning occurred when I first heard "Tarkus" by Emerson, Lake, and Palmer. I was struck by the power of the suspended chords that Keith Emerson was using (sus2, sus4). I thought it was a great sound, so I spent time learning that. Instead of learning the actual piece of music (which really wasn't my style), I would play the chords that I liked and I practiced finding those chords in all keys. Once I was comfortable with the chords, I would try writing my own short piece using those chords.

Another example is from Genesis and Tony Banks's wonderful writing, which emphasized using different triads over unusual bass notes. Todd Rundgren also used a similar type of writing, but with a different result. This method of practice can help with technique, improvisation, and also composition. With regards to composition, I like to write short pieces that incorporate some new concept that I had just discovered. I remember being taught a lesson about minor second intervals, and once I had heard the interval plus a piece that used those intervals, I was instructed to write my own piece that incorporated a similar sound.

When I am preparing for a live performance, I have a unique approach. I have a unique background for synthesis since I came from a classical background. Both of my hands are equally strong, technique-wise, which is unusual. Since I am always so interested in learning about everything that a synthesizer can possibly do, often I want to get as much out of the instrument in front of me as I can. I'm more interested in maximizing the sonic potential of one keyboard rather than expanding that potential across a lot of different keyboards. If I move on stage now during a DT performance, it's more for show than anything else. The majority of my performance is going to be at my main keyboard. The reality of current technology is that modern keyboards are very powerful, and they are capable of doing much more than people think. Many people love to use sounds from many different keyboards, and I am much the same way, and I will use lots of different keyboards when we record, but when it comes to the live setting, I am able to produce all of those sounds out of the instrument of my choice. I can either recreate sounds with the available on-board patches, or sometimes I'll bring in samples. This allows me to be more focused and control everything from a single keyboard using my "magic" pedal. This pedal is actually just a switch pedal that switches between my various "setups" or "combinations" in the correct order for a show. Sometimes my combinations are very complicated with multi-layered sounds that are different between the hands, but some combinations are simpler. Overall, I use literally hundreds of sounds over the course of a single show.

Another important aspect to live performance is learning how to stay calm. To this day, I still get nervous before I play a show, usually before the first show on a tour when I'm not as used to the live setting. Even so, I have various skills I use to calm down. One thing you don't want to do is think about the part that's coming up. If you start to concern yourself with the next section before you've reached it, you're almost guaranteed to screw it up. Try to stay in the moment. I try to sing or hum along internally with the music that's going on to keep my mind focused on what's happening right then. This is probably a good idea with life as well: stay in the moment!

Studio preparation is another story. In DT, it's a really fun environment because, often, the drums and guitars are already done and it's a chance for me to bring all my keyboards into the control room. This is an opposite approach to my live rig because I want to have all sorts of sounds and inspirations readily available. Oftentimes, a particular sound can inspire a particular part during the writing process. During the recording of Systematic Chaos, we got turned on to the Korg Radias, and a lot of those patches inspired what was going on. I also like to use a lot of software and plugins. Some of the possibilities that are offered by soft synths open new doors to how we can control and create sound. Oftentimes these libraries, like an entire orchestral soft-synth library, go so much further than any hardware sound would ever go. The world of keyboards and technology evolves so fast that it's fun and important to keep up with all of it. Just recently during my space jam with Richard Lainhart, I opened the show playing my iPhone using a synthesizer that my friend Zach Gage developed, called SynthPond. It's a 3-D sound-making program where you're spinning these reactors and effectors around a central point, and you can make them orbit and do all sorts of cool stuff.

How do you approach practicing/preparing all the material for an upcoming tour?

It's always a stressful time leading up to a tour. I have to remember a lot of old music as well as learn all the new music that we will perform. I have to dig up old files of sounds and refresh myself on older songs. I often make a playlist on my iPod to listen to all the tunes I will be relearning. I'm also fortunate because these days, I'll have pretty much all the music transcribed, so I can always go back and look at the transcription to refresh myself. We're all very lucky to have the luxury of having a book like this written by Chris Romero, who probably knows my musical life better than anyone out there. When you see the notes and fingerings, it's all very dialed in to what I'm actually doing and thinking.

A lot of times in the studio, not only will I play a ton of synthesizers, but I'm usually not thinking about how I'll pull it off live. Maybe I'll play a wild unison lead with John, but then I'll play some chords at the same time. Then it comes time to play live, and I have the challenge of figuring out how to pull it all off. In some cases, there are also other rhythm guitar parts that I have to cover live because John recorded a rhythm track but also a lead or unison track. In "The Ministry of Lost Souls," I have to cover John's rhythm part during a harmonized run that we play together. So I'm playing the run in the right hand, but I have a rhythm guitar sound in the lower octaves so that my left hand can fill in that whole sonic space. A similar thing happens at the end of "In the Presence of Enemies Pt. 1," where I am playing chords and covering a rhythm guitar part in my left hand while playing a wild run with John in the right hand. We've always been a little crazy in that sense. Sometimes while writing in the studio, we'll think, "How are we going to pull this off live?" But that is part of the way we strive to constantly challenge ourselves. It keeps us on our toes and keeps us feeling vital and on top of our game. I think that's what it takes to be a great player – that desire to always want to move forward and get to the next level. I don't know where that comes from, maybe it's a love for music, maybe it's for the way it feels when our technique is really on. There's a feeling to nailing a part and to realizing things are in your control and are the way you want them. When we can execute a line perfectly, that's an incredible thing.

What are your major influences? Favorite literature?

My favorite classical music to play is written by Chopin. I think he wrote some of the most beautiful piano music. I'm attracted to composers that really understand the instruments that they're writing for. I think that someone like Chopin or Debussy really understood the way a piano sounds or resonates and would write their passages to make the instrument speak and be very beautiful. I also love Bach. I can relate to Bach in the same way I can relate to some of the more progressive rock stuff I do, especially when I go for a Gentle Giant sound, because they used a lot of counterpoint in their music, and I was influenced by that a lot.

With rock music, I'm very influenced by the progressive elements of rock. Bands like Yes, King Crimson, Gentle Giant, and Genesis are all strong influences on me. As a progressive artist, I also like to listen to "cutting edge" music. For me this is current electronic music. Artists like Richard Devine, Murcof, Boards of Canada, Aphex Twin, Autechre, Square Pusher, and Kiln are really on top of pushing the boundaries of music. Some people might not love the actual music, but you have to admit that these people are forward thinkers, and they're doing things that have not been done yet. I just heard the premiere of Steven Wilson's new solo album, *Insurgentes*, and it was unbelievable. Steven really knows how to make his sonic vision turn into reality.

What is the "Continuum"? How did you get involved with it and how do you use it in your rig?

I had been thinking for some years now about wanting an instrument where, not only could you play the pitch like on a keyboard, but you could also play the pitch and then slide to another and be able to do vibrato like on a violin or guitar. I was talking to friends and dreaming about this type of instrument. One day, I got a call from my neighbor, Richard Lainhart, who asked if I'd read the article in Keyboard magazine about the "Haken Continuum" because he thought it looked like exactly what I had dreamt about. After spending some time reading the article, I realized that this was the instrument I had been searching for. I quickly contacted Lippold Haken, the designer of the Continuum, who is a wonderful, interesting, smart, laid-back genius in his own right. He's a professor of technology at the University of Illinois. He was interested in my case because I wanted to use the Continuum in a rock setting, and up to that point, the instrument had been mostly used by academic people for their music. I immediately liked the Continuum once I started playing it, and I began to work closely with Lippold to develop new features for the instrument. One of the new features became very important for me to use it effectively in a rock setting. We needed to add a sort of pitch quantization that "rounded" the pitch even if my finger was slightly off center of the actual key on the controller. When I slide to another note and stop, the Continuum will automatically round the pitch to the nearest diatonic step. This rounding speed is also adjustable depending on the type of sound you want to have. Mostly I use the Continuum for my heavier, rock sounds, which I trigger off a V-synth.

Volume pedals for Continuum and Lap Steel
Photo © Atsushi Sato

Roland V Synths triggered by Continuum
Photo © Atsushi Sato

Photos © Atsushi Sato

Photo © Atsushi Sato

Photo © Janet Balmer

Photo © Darko Boehringer

Photos © Darko Boehringer

Lead Notation Guide

Whenever lead notation is shown, a non-parenthetical note always indicates a key that is physically played on the keyboard, while a note in parentheses indicates the sounding note, i.e. what you hear. The lines above the staff show the movement of the pitch wheel, or, where indicated, the movement on a ribbon controller. The numbers above the lines (or, occasionally below the lines for downward bends) represent the size of a bend in terms of whole steps. So, "1" means to bend a whole step, while "1/2" means to bend only a half step. Vibrato lines indicate that you should add vibrato to that note by quickly moving the pitch wheel up and down in small motions.

In example A, this notation instructs you to physically play C for a quarter note, bend up a whole step to D for a quarter note, and then release the bend on beat 3.

Example B is similar to A, except you only bend a half step from B to C. The vibrato line instead of a straight line over the bent note C indicates that you should vibrato the C before releasing the bend back to B on beat 4.

Example C shows a melody that is played while constantly holding the pitch wheel at the top position. You begin by playing C and bending to D on beat 2. On beat 3, you physically play D and F as eighth notes, but since you have the pitch wheel up a whole step, you hear E and G instead. You release the bend on beat 4 back to F.

When bends do not have a rhythmical value associated with them, the physically played note is shown as a grace note preceding the parenthetical sounding note. In example D, you play D on beat 1, then you play C on beat 2 but instantly bend it up a whole step to D. Quickly release the bend to play an actual D again on beat 3, then instantly bend a C to D on beat 4.

I use the pitch wheel to scoop into notes, as well as to dive off at the end of a phrase. Scoops do not have an exact pitch value associated with them, so they are shown as two lines creating a V shape (as shown leading into beat 2). Dives are shown as a single diagonal line pointing down and right.

In some songs, I'll use my left hand to play a few notes in a lead or fast run. Wherever hand switches occur in a part shown on a single staff, the "L" and "R" letters below the staff indicate the starting point for using the left or right hand, respectively. (Example F)

Pitch Bending

One of the great discoveries for me along the way was the pitch wheel. Pitch bending nowadays often involves a joystick (like it or not) instead of a wheel. Although I grew up with the traditional Minimoog-style wheel, many of the instruments I play now have a joystick in its place. On the Korg Oasys, there are some great advantages of the joystick operation for expression. The joystick not only goes left and right for pitch, but also forward and back, and at the same time! That allows me to introduce cool feedback-like tones of all shapes and sizes as I am jamming my leads.

Kevin Moore, the original Dream Theater keyboardist, will get credit here for playing an awesome lead in the song "Take the Time." What I like about it is how he used the idea of playing a key, bending it up to a pitch, and then repeating the note on the actual key of the pitch—like the first measure of this etude, "Bending Time," where the note B is bent up to a C#, followed by a C# played on the actual C# key. It's a cool effect. If you can get through this etude, you too will be a master at this technique. You will also be smiling a lot!

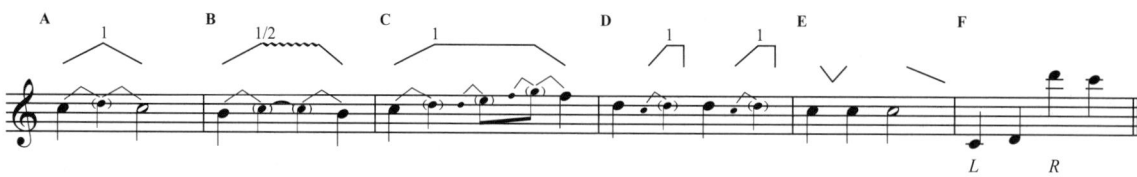

BENDING TIME

By JORDAN RUDESS

TAKE THE TIME

Words and Music by JAMES LABRIE, KEVIN MOORE,
JOHN MYUNG, JOHN PETRUCCI, and MIKE PORTNOY

©1992 WB MUSIC CORP., and YTSE JAMS, INC.
All Rights administered by WB MUSIC CORP.
All Rights Reserved

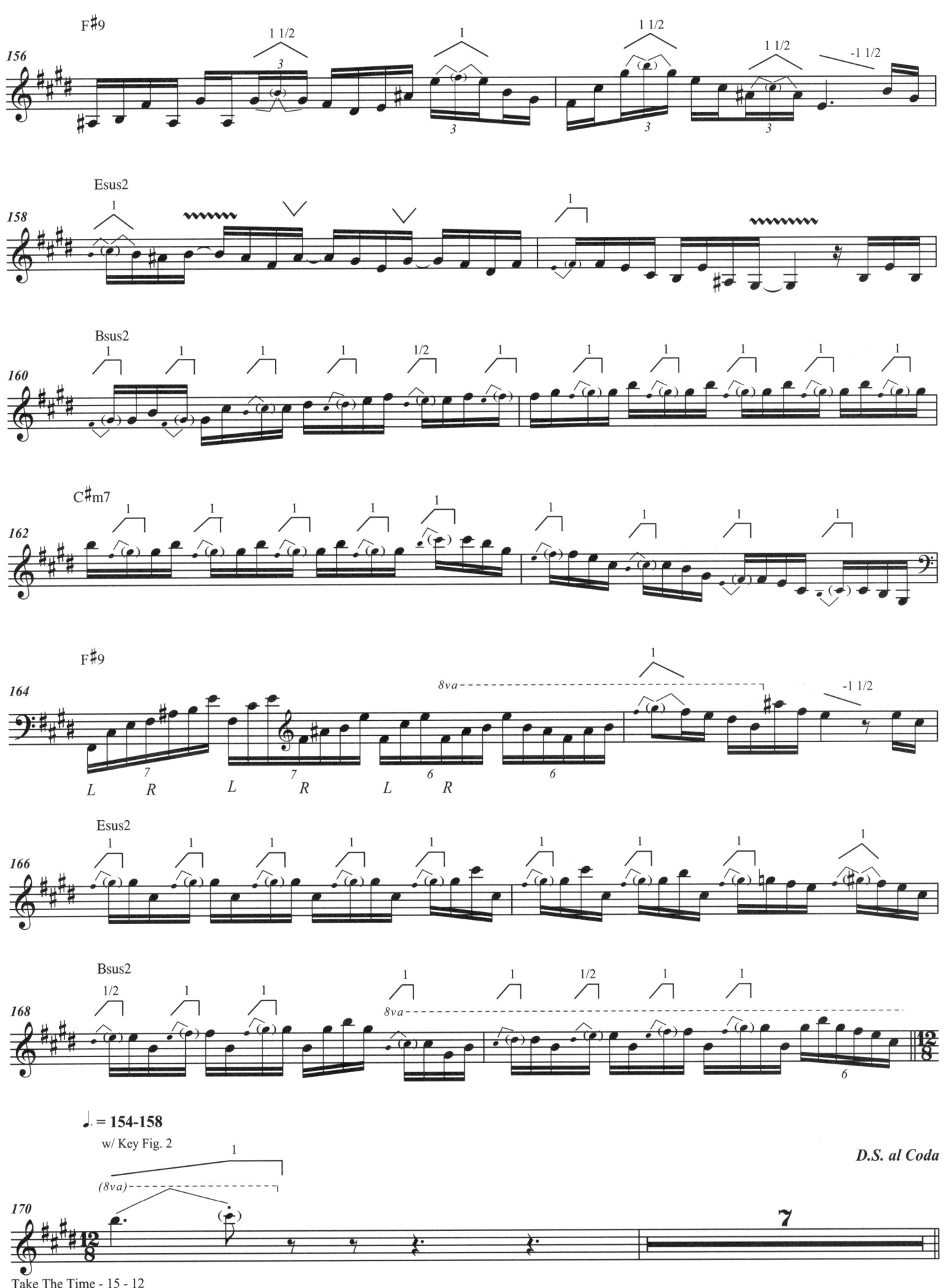

Take The Time - 15 - 12

Photo © Atsushi Sato

Arpeggiated Chord Inversions

This exercise is all about inversions and getting through them smoothly. The beautiful thing here is that we spent a lot of time on the fingering, which will take the guesswork out of it for you, and hopefully get you on the right track for your keyboard future!

It will benefit you greatly to be able to quickly put your hands on any chord in its various inversions. I used to spend a lot of time just sitting at the piano getting used to playing whatever chord popped into my head in every inversion I could find! *Space Dye Vest* is a very moody song, so the chords lent themselves well to further adventure.

For those of you who are more advanced, how about playing this etude in E minor as well?

Enjoy.

The inspiration for this etude is from the chords of "Space Dye Vest," which follows on page 34.

SPACETUDE VEST

By JORDAN RUDESS

SPACE-DYE VEST

By KEVIN MOORE

© 1994 WB MUSIC CORP., and Ytse Jams, INC.
All Rights Administered by WB MUSIC CORP.
All Rights Reserved

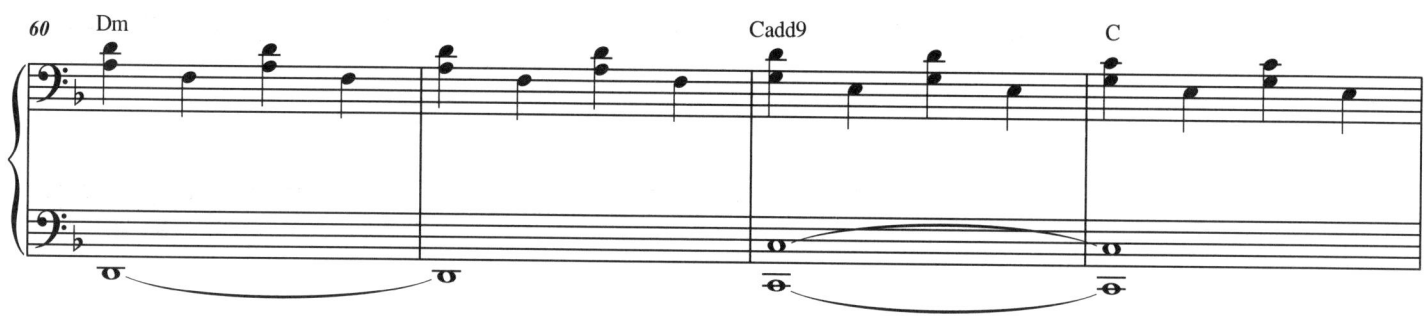
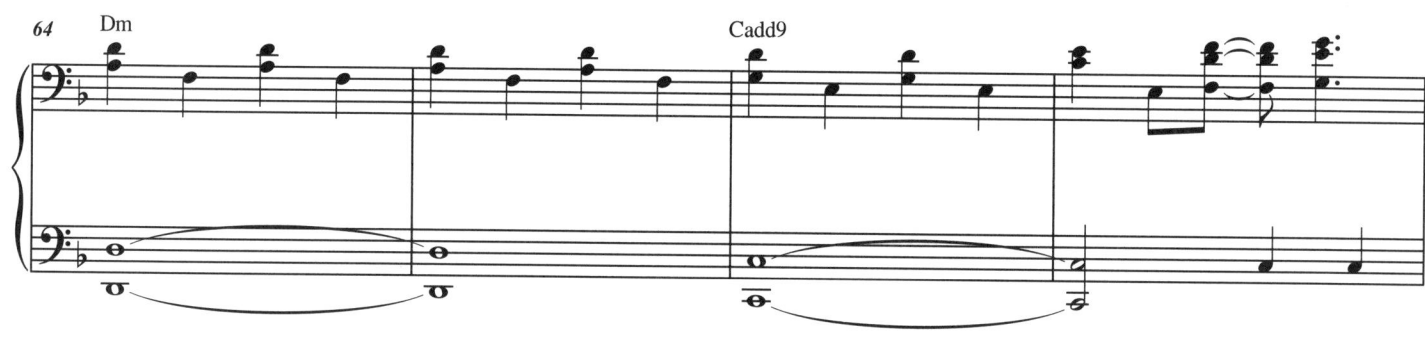
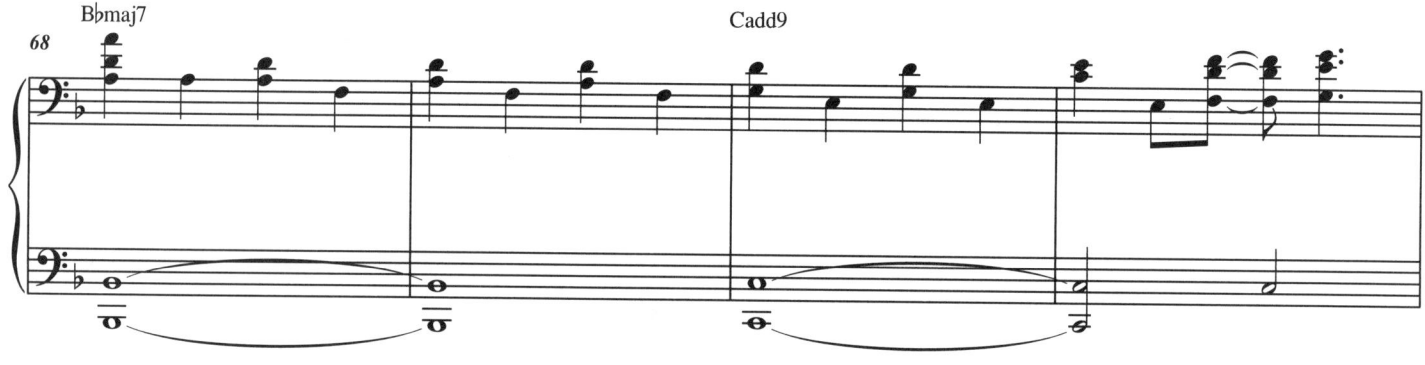
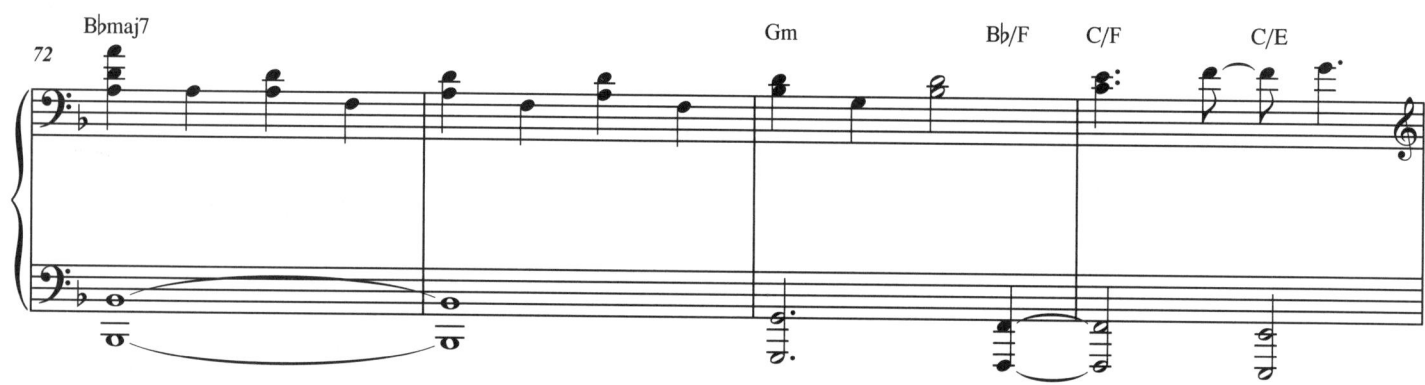

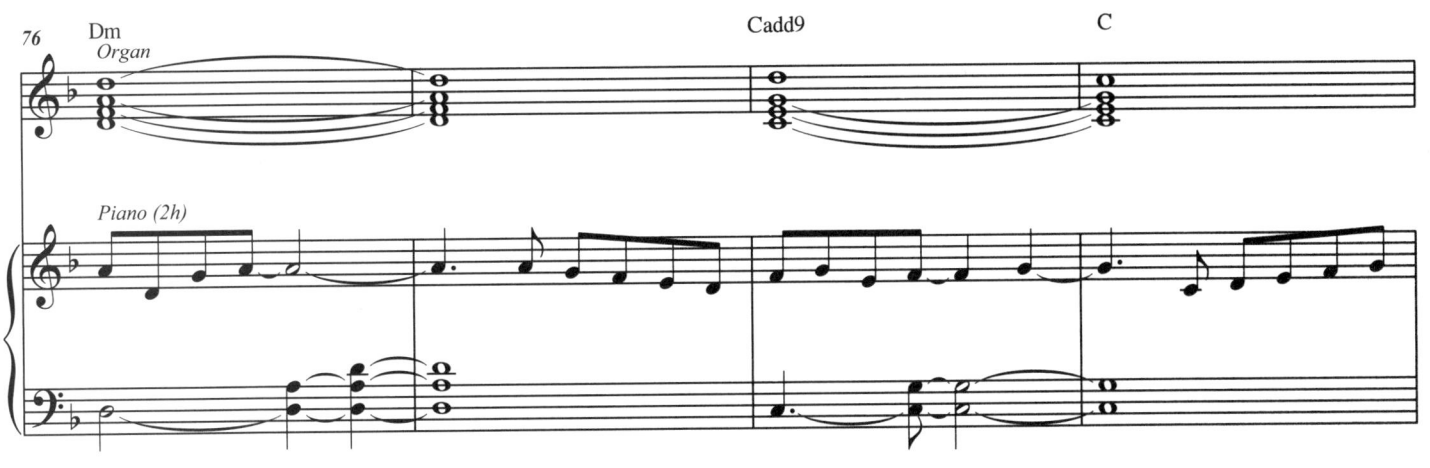
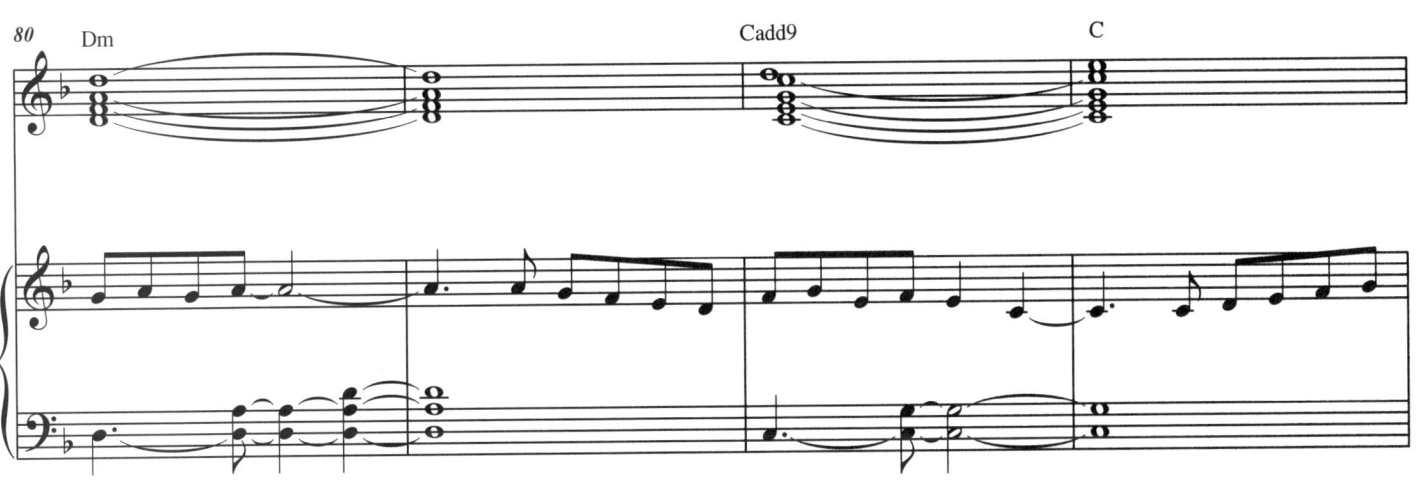
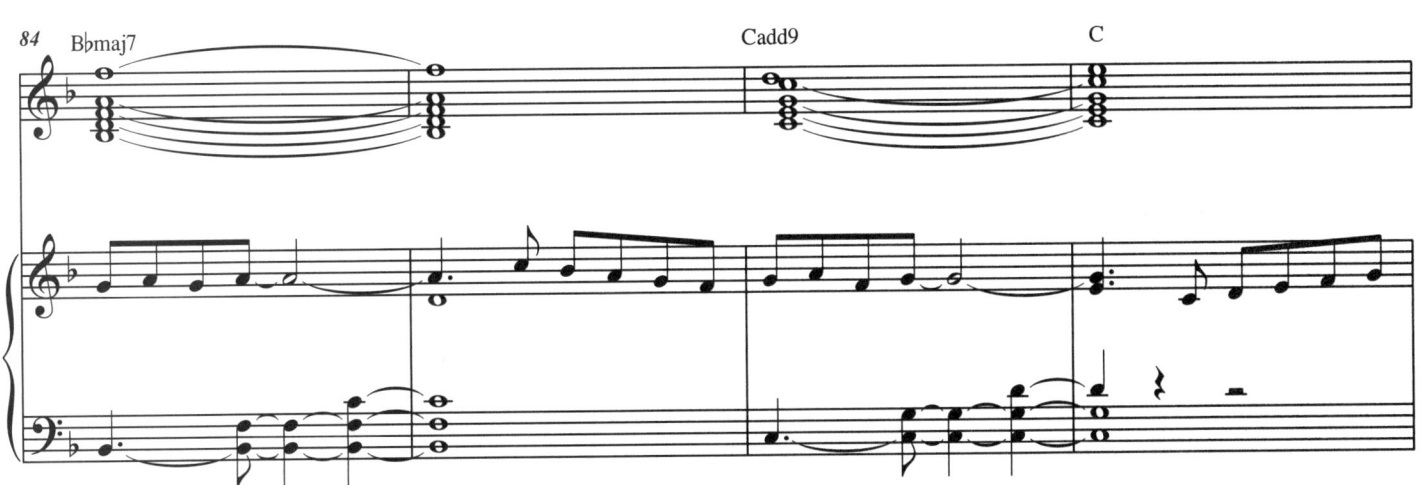

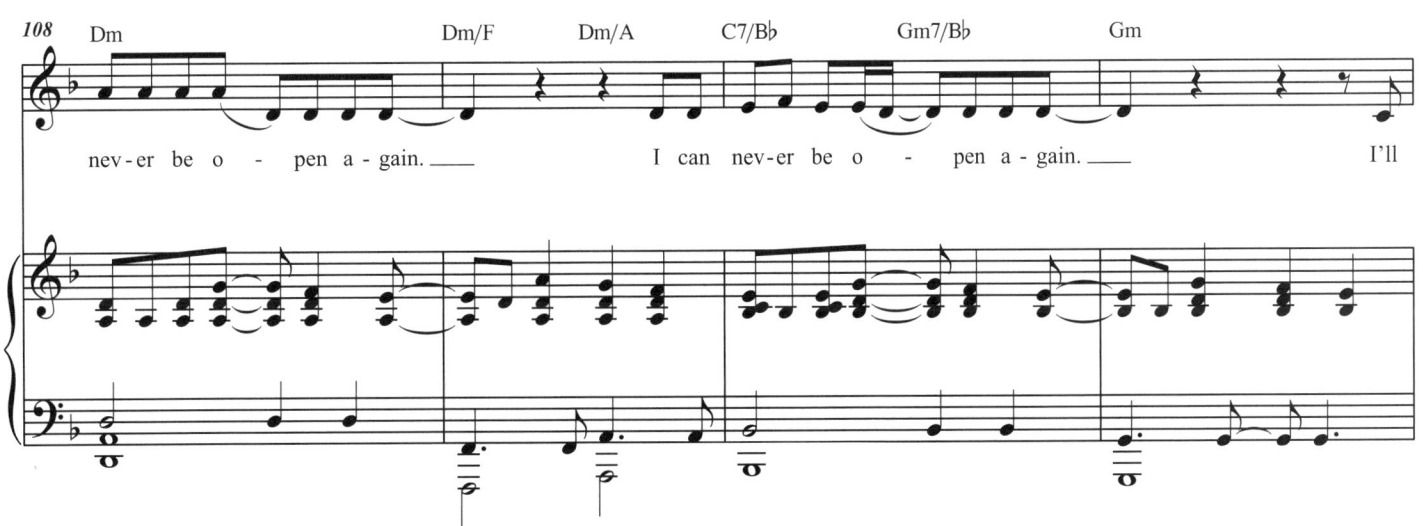

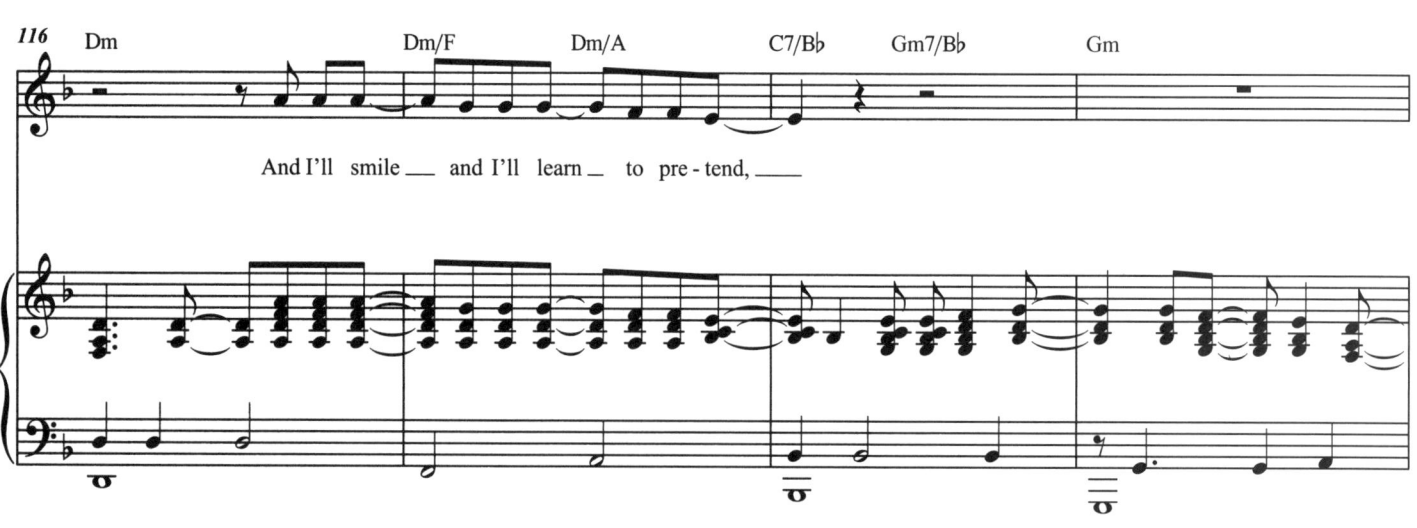
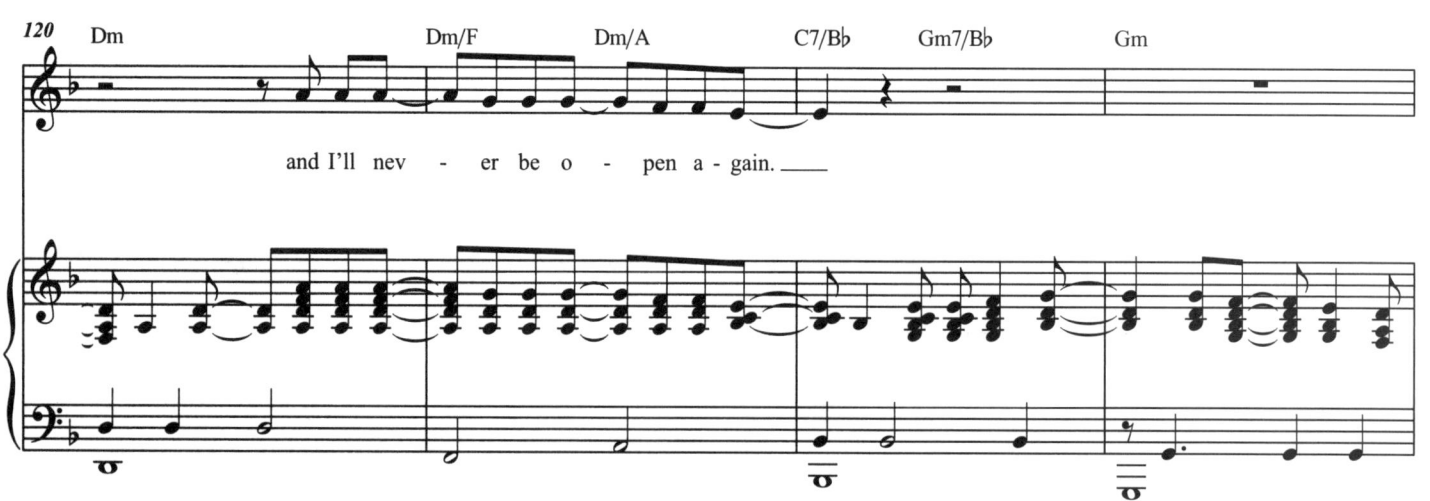

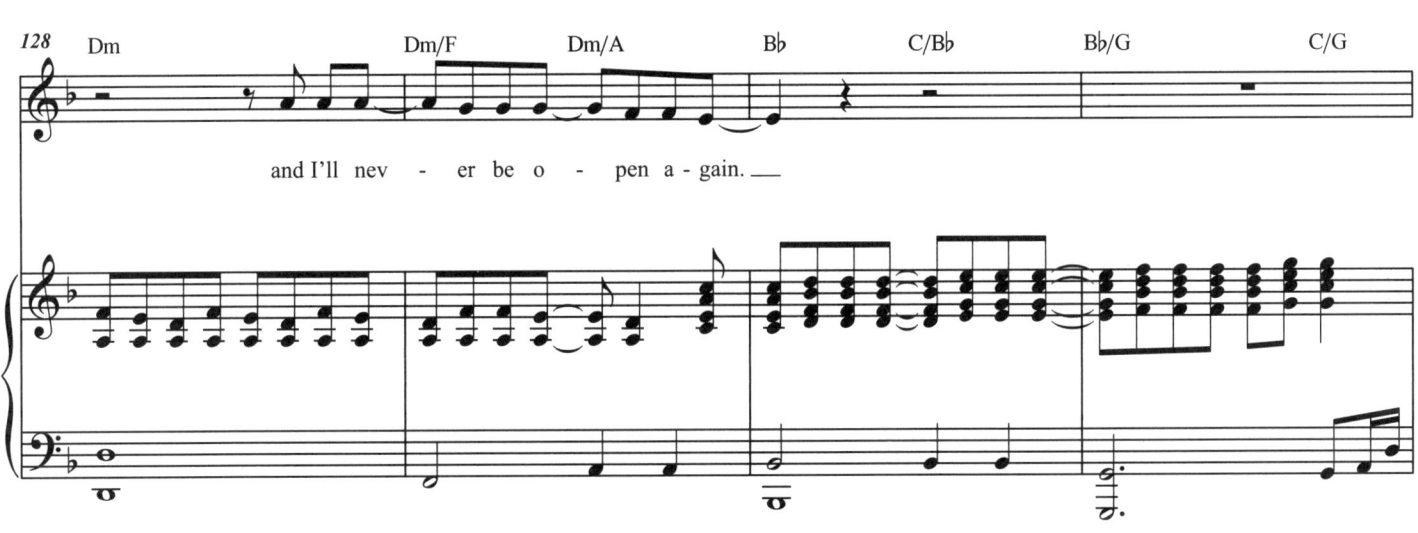
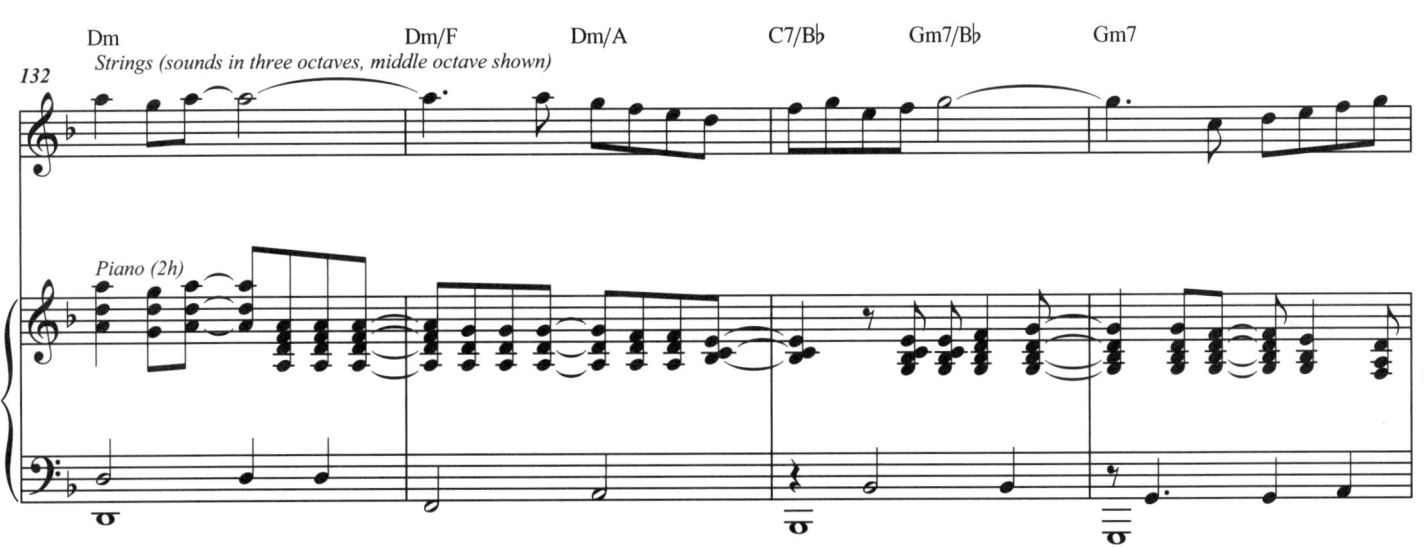

Repeated Figures with Shifting Accent Patterns

I love when there is a repeating series of notes, and every time it wraps around, the accent shifts to a different note. You will see exactly what this keyboard madness is all about once you dive in to this etude. I'm a big believer in this type of finger and mind training. It also sounds cool, which is why I'm offering it to you!

It's based on the passage at the end of Home, where the band stops and there is a keyboard moment that introduces the very ethnic-sounding sitar and tabla riff. If you ever need to clear your mind of the doldrums or pressures of modern life, I strongly recommend spending time on this etude. Practice it very slowly at first.

The inspiration for this etude is from measure 261 (page 64) of "Home" from *Metropolis, Part 2: Scenes from a Memory.*

DANCING HOME

By JORDAN RUDESS

SCENE SIX: HOME

Music by JAMES LABRIE, JOHN MYUNG,
JOHN PETRUCCI, MIKE PORTNOY, and JORDAN RUDESS
Lyrics by MIKE PORTNOY

© 1999 WB MUSIC CORP., and YTSE JAMS, INC.
All Rights Administered by WB MUSIC CORP.
All Rights Reserved

50

Scene Six: Home - 18 - 3

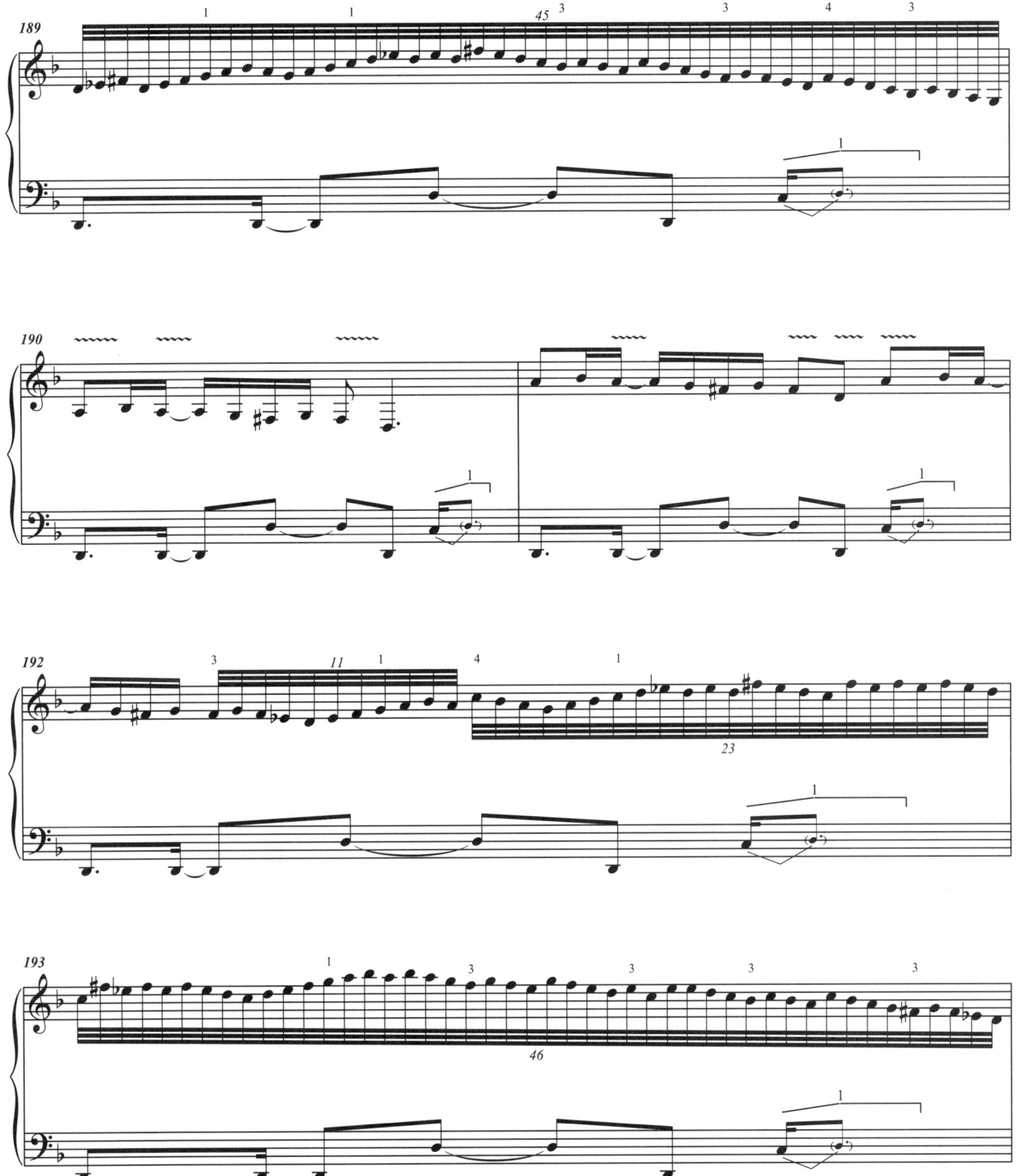

Two-Handed Playing of Wide-Range Melodic Leads

This exercise focuses on the very important keyboard technique of being able to quickly switch between your two hands when playing a single-note line.

Developing this technique frees up your creativity by making you realize that you don't need to limit your solo lines to what you can do with only your right hand. Now, don't take this as an excuse to "cheat" on those passages that could and should be played with one hand! This technique is for when notes occur in different ranges and would be extremely difficult or impossible to be played with one hand.

I think you will find that this one feels really cool to play when you "get it." As with all of these exercises, it is not only a lesson in finger technique, but also patience.

Have fun!

The inspiration for this etude is from measure 247 (page 81) of "Blind Faith" from *Six Degrees of Inner Turbulence*.

HAND FAITH

By JORDAN RUDESS

BLIND FAITH

Music by JOHN MYUNG, JOHN PETRUCCI,
MIKE PORTNOY, and JORDAN RUDESS
Lyrics by JAMES LABRIE

*Improvise freely with lead, primary notes are D, G, A, C.
Part of the line is shown here to demonstrate the concept.
End the run on the D shown in measure 3 and continue as written.

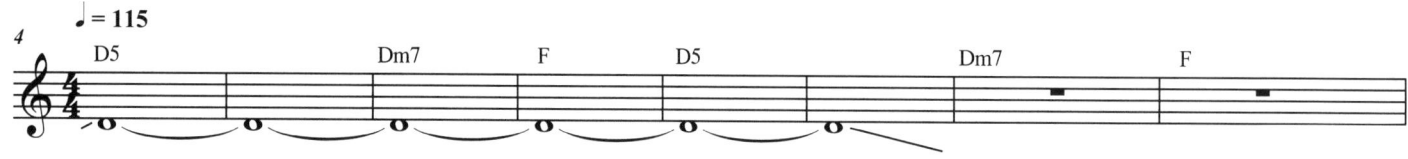

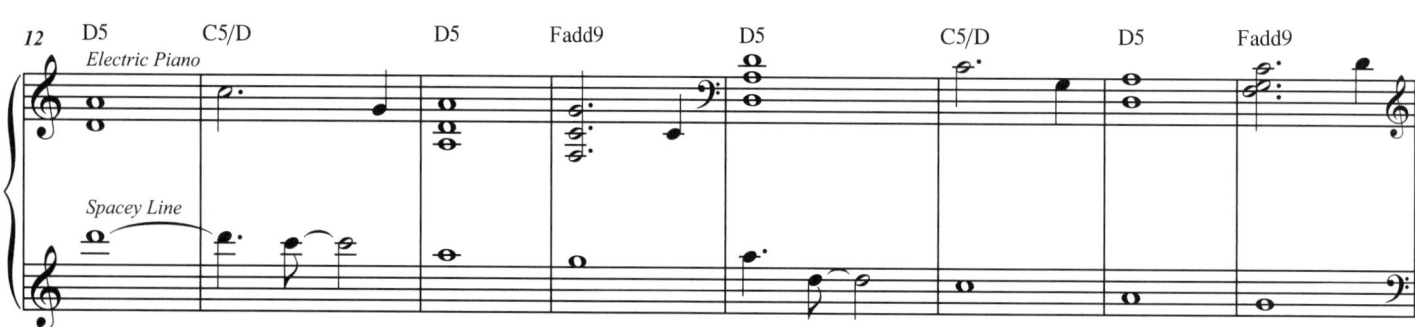

©2001 WB MUSIC CORP., and Ytse Jams, INC.
All Rights Administered by WB MUSIC CORP.
All Rights Reserved

Blind Faith - 18 - 11

Blind Faith - 18 - 14

84

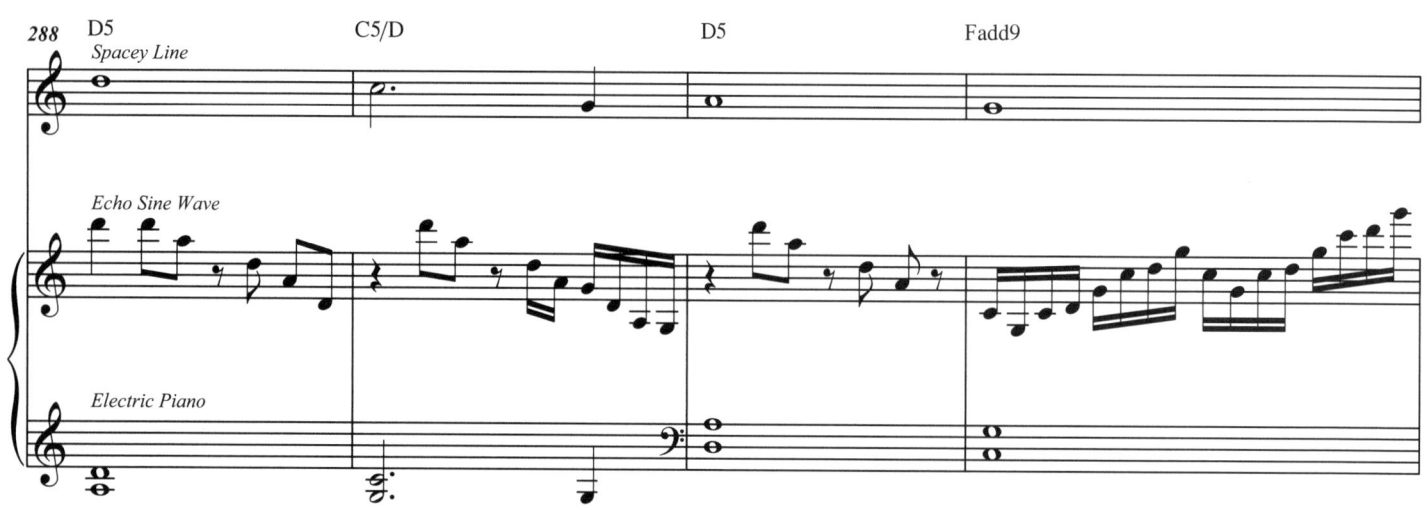

Blind Faith - 18 - 17

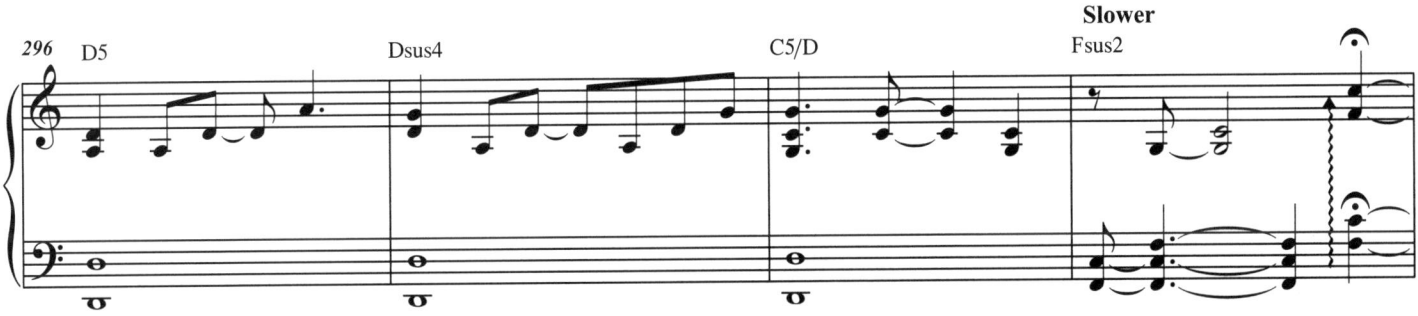

Synchronization of Left and Right Hands Playing Parallel Figures

Keeping the left hand and right hand in sync is something we all work on all the time. It's at these points in the live show that I usually settle down and be as still mentally (and even physically) as possible. When the biggest challenges come up, I need to be at my calmest.

Here is an etude that you can practice being calm with. It's like the Rudess version of Czerny. Watch out for the changing key signatures, which happen every four measures. For the ultimate challenge, see if you can have a conversation with your friend while playing this!

The inspiration for this etude is from measure 125 (page 98) of "Honor Thy Father" from *Train of Thought*.

HONOR YOUR TEACHER

By JORDAN RUDESS

HONOR THY FATHER

Music by JOHN MYUNG, JOHN PETRUCCI,
MIKE PORTNOY, and JORDAN RUDESS
Lyrics by MIKE PORTNOY

*Mike plays a 6/8 feel next four measures.

©2003 YTSE JAMS, INC.
All Rights Administered by WB MUSIC CORP.
All Rights Reserved

92

Honor Thy Father - 18 - 5

98

Photo © Janet Balmer

Alternation between Triplet and Sixteenth-Note Rhythms in Lead Lines

Just in case you were cheating on the "Hand Faith" exercise, I created this one to bring you back into focus! Not only is the challenge to play fast and smooth arpeggios of every shape and size, but the real focus is on the rhythmic element of the lines.

Notice how it quickly goes from straight sixteenth notes to triplets of sixteenths. It might be a little tricky to make that change smoothly at first. That's cool—that's definitely the hard part, and the reason that I created this. You've heard this tip before… "Turn on that metronome!" Make sure that you are not moving your elbow and body around too much. You don't want to have any wasted movements here!

The inspiration for this etude is from measure 187 (page 123) of "Octavarium" from the *Octavarium* album.

OCTAWIZARD

By JORDAN RUDESS

OCTAVARIUM

Words and Music by JAMES LABRIE, JOHN MYUNG, JOHN PETRUCCI, MIKE PORTNOY, and JORDAN RUDESS

©2005 WB MUSIC CORP., YTSE JAMS, INC., WARNER-TAMERLANE PUBLISHING CORP., and KEY WIZ MUSIC
All Rights on behalf of Itself and YTSE JAMS, INC. administered by WB MUSIC CORP.
All Rights on behalf of Itself and KEY WIZ MUSIC administered by WARNER-TAMERLANE PUBLISHING CORP.
All Rights Reserved

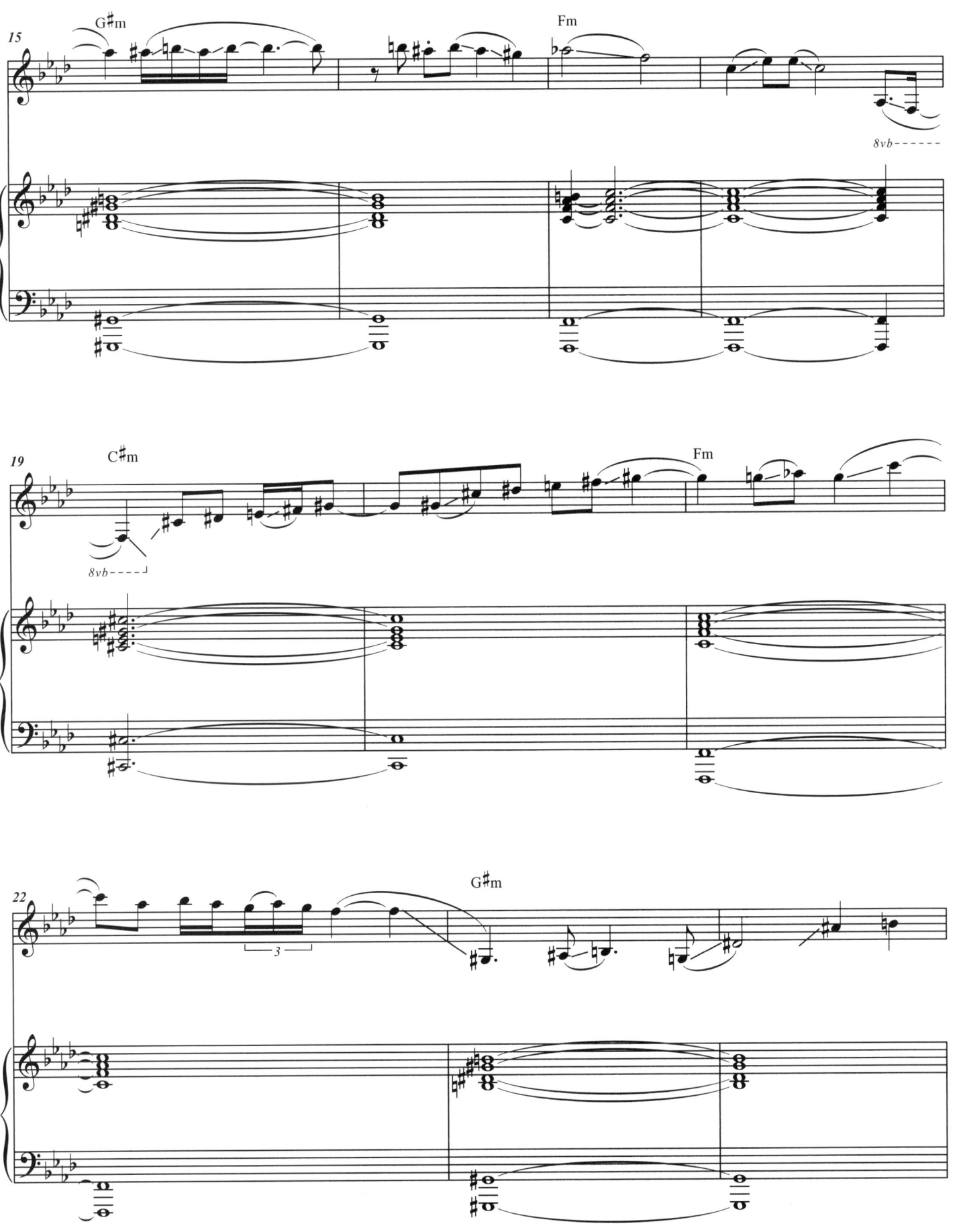

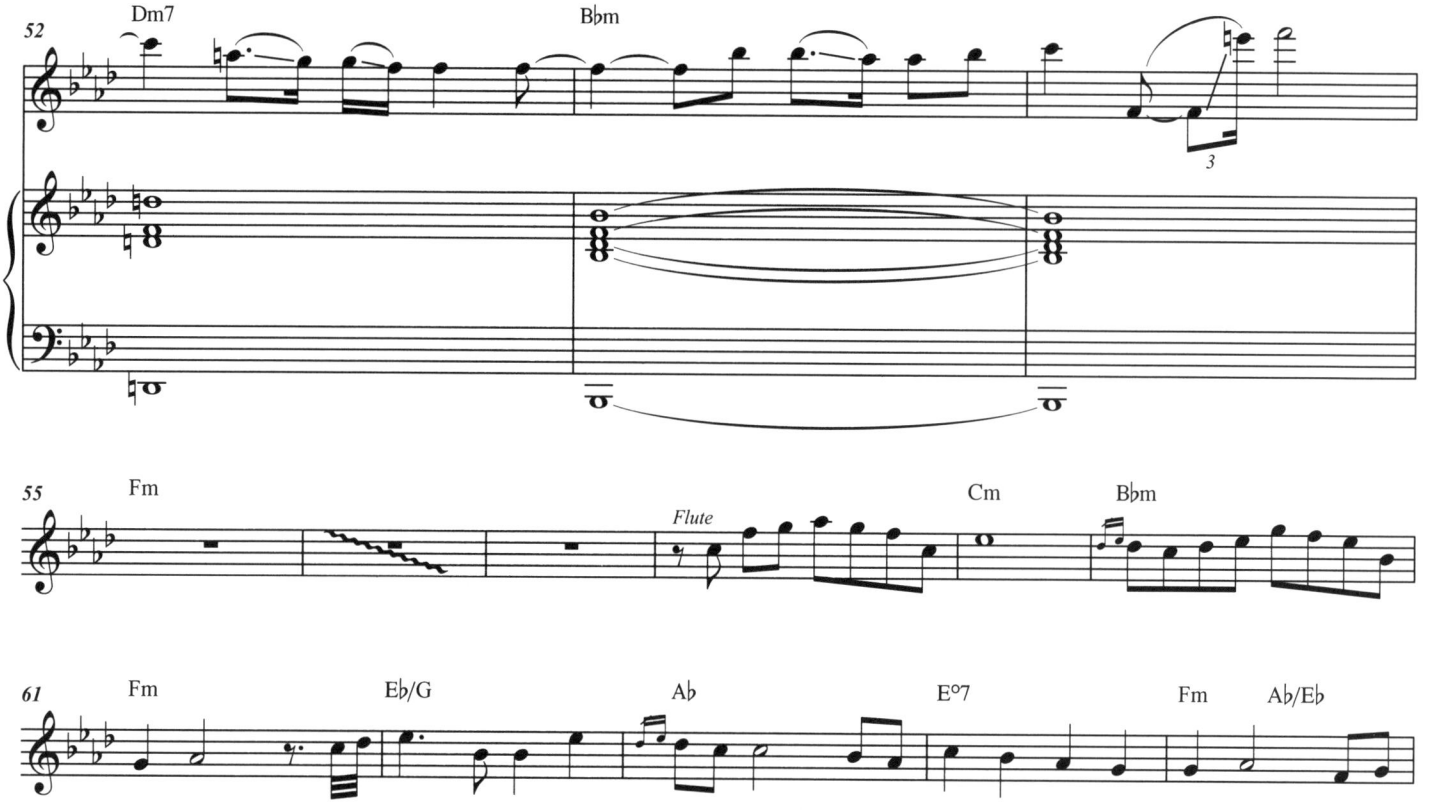

I. Someone Like Him

I nev-er want-ed to be-come some-one like him, so se-cure.

II. Medicate (Awakening)

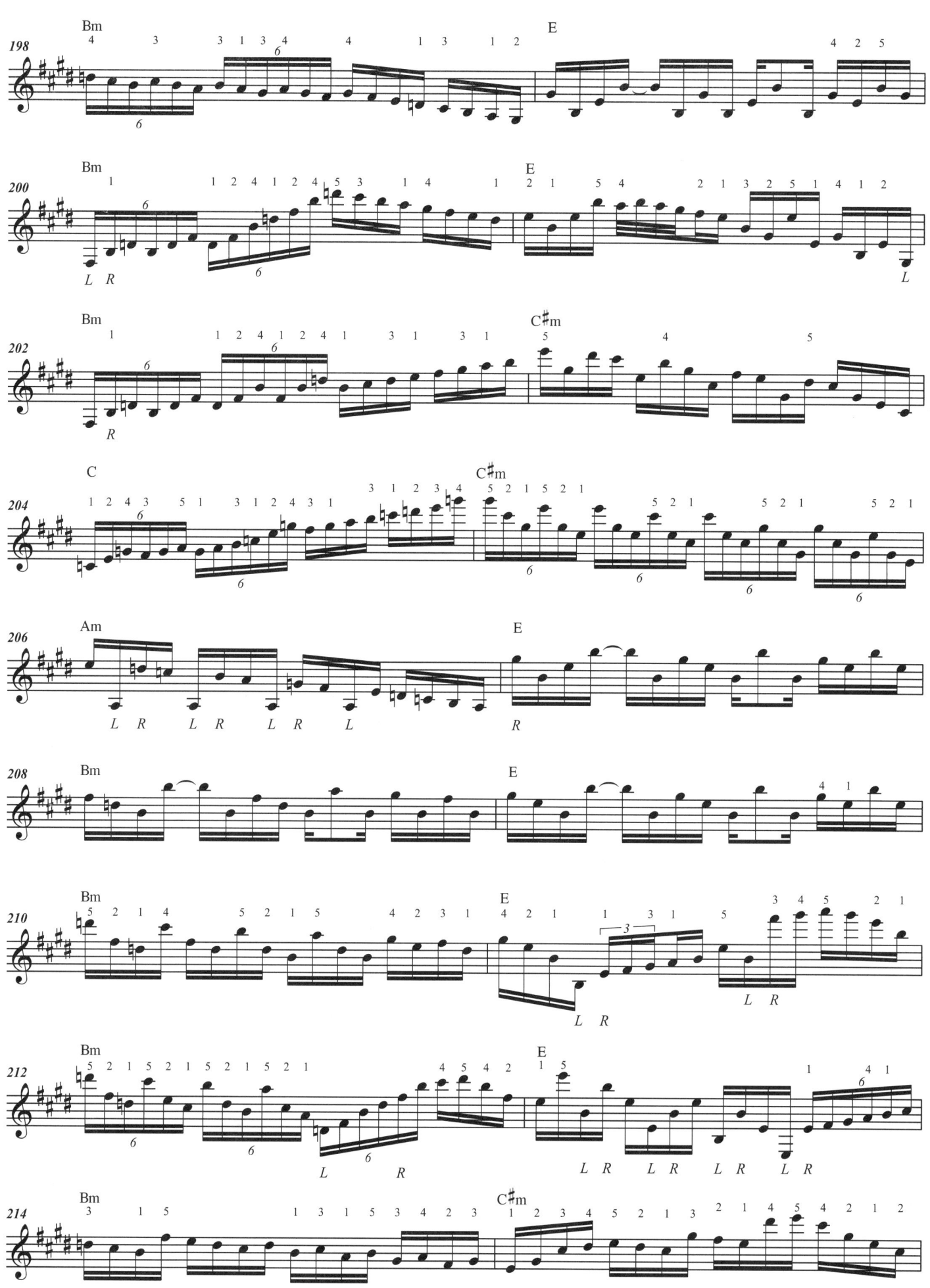

III. Full Circle

IV. Intervals

V. Razor's Edge

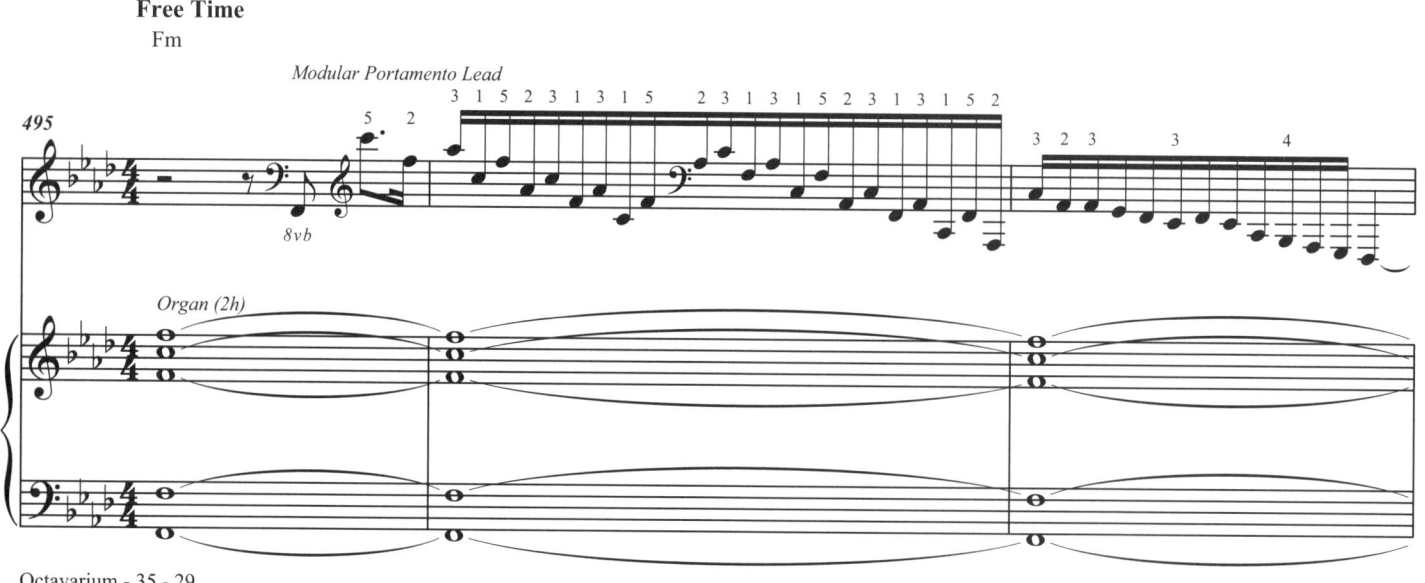

Photo © Janet Balmer

Extremely Rapid Passages

This is an etude designed to develop what we in Dream Theater call the "Bee" technique. The technique involves notes that are very close together, moving in rapid succession. It's a bit of a brain (and finger) twister, but really worth your time and effort. Follow the fingerings we included very carefully. There will be no cheating!! Mixed into the fun at measure 11 is another "fun" technique that I call mirroring. Altogether, your challenge is clear. Take your time with this, and remember to breathe.

The inspiration for this etude is from measure 58 (page 151) of "In the Presence of Enemies, Pt. 1" from *Systematic Chaos*.

BEE ENEMY

By JORDAN RUDESS

IN THE PRESENCE OF ENEMIES - PART I
The Heretic and The Dark Master
I. Prelude

Music by JAMES LABRIE, JOHN MYUNG,
JOHN PETRUCCI, MIKE PORTNOY, and JORDAN RUDESS
Lyrics by JOHN PETRUCCI

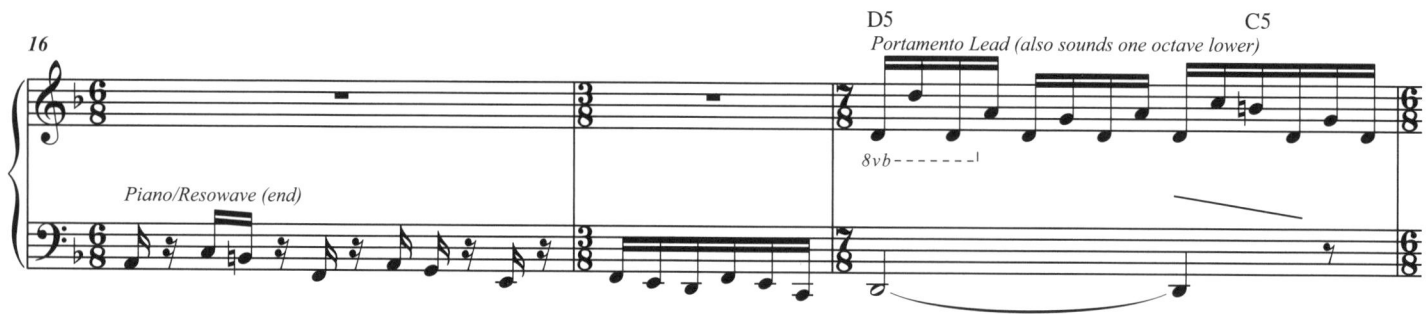

©2007 WB MUSIC CORP., YTSE JAMS, INC., WARNER-TAMERLANE PUBLISHING CORP., and KEY WIZ MUSIC
All Rights on behalf of Itself and YTSE JAMS, INC. administered by WB MUSIC CORP.
All Rights on behalf of Itself and KEY WIZ MUSIC administered by WARNER-TAMERLANE PUBLISHING CORP.
All Rights Reserved

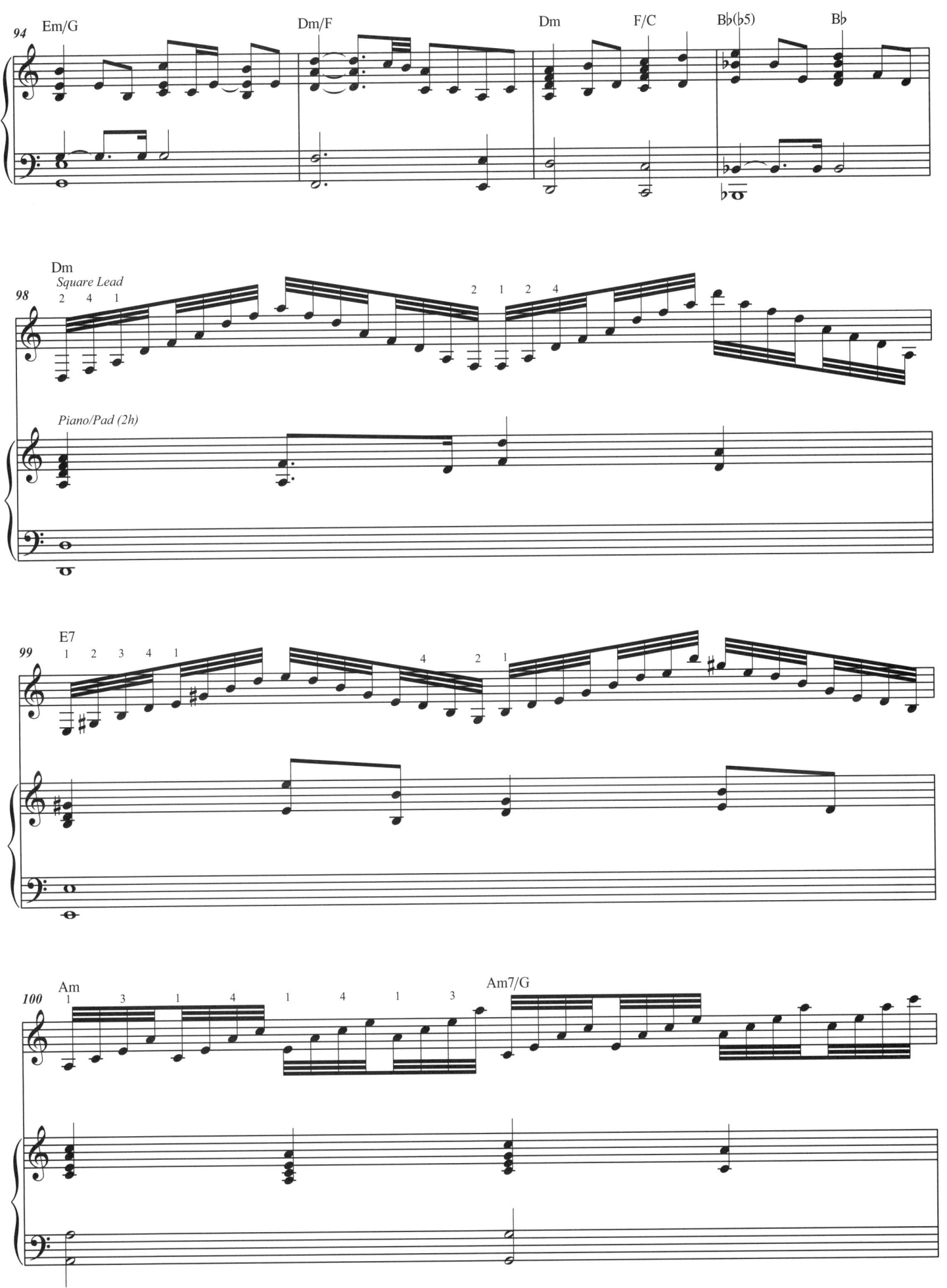

154

II. Resurrection

158

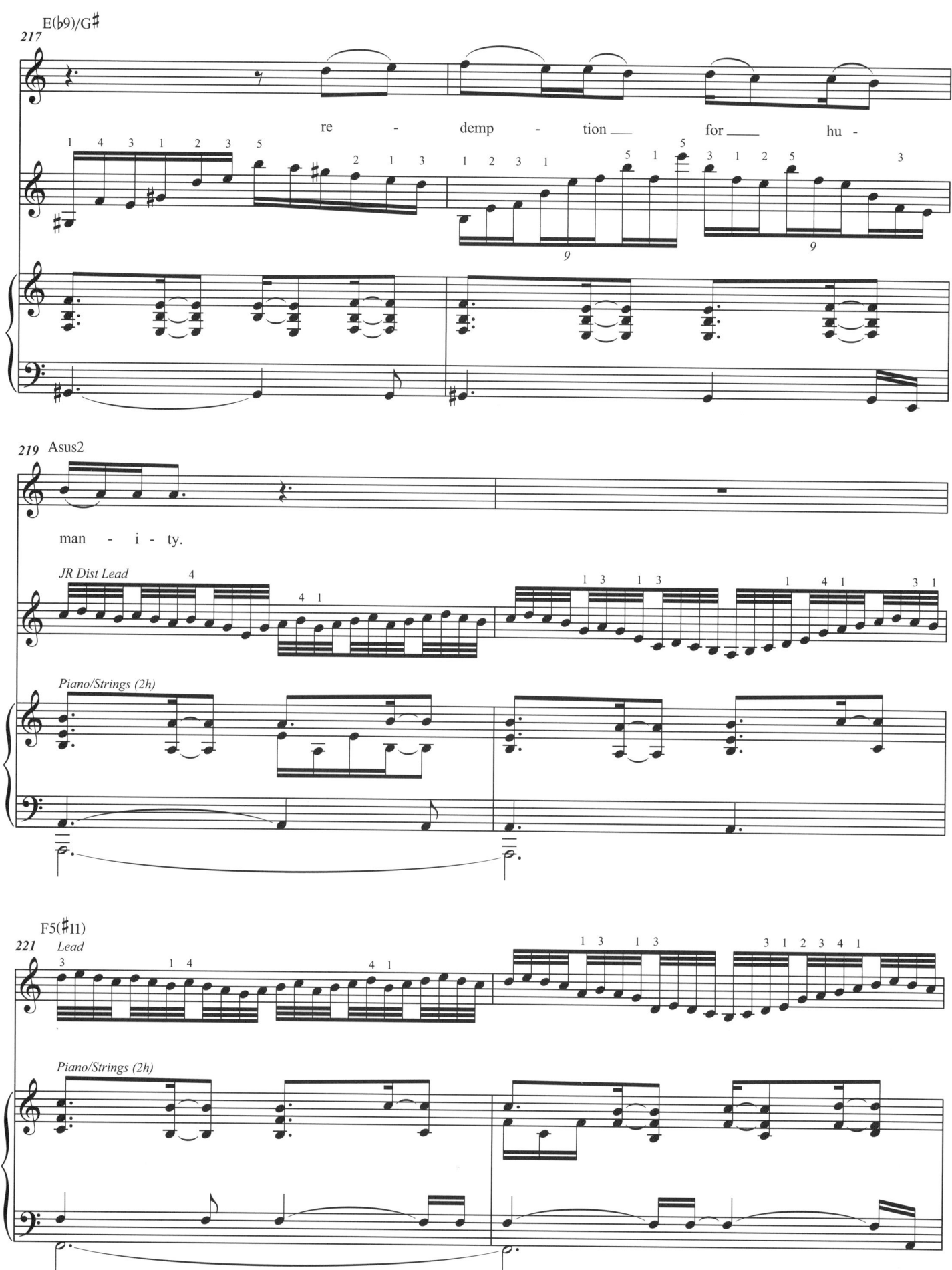

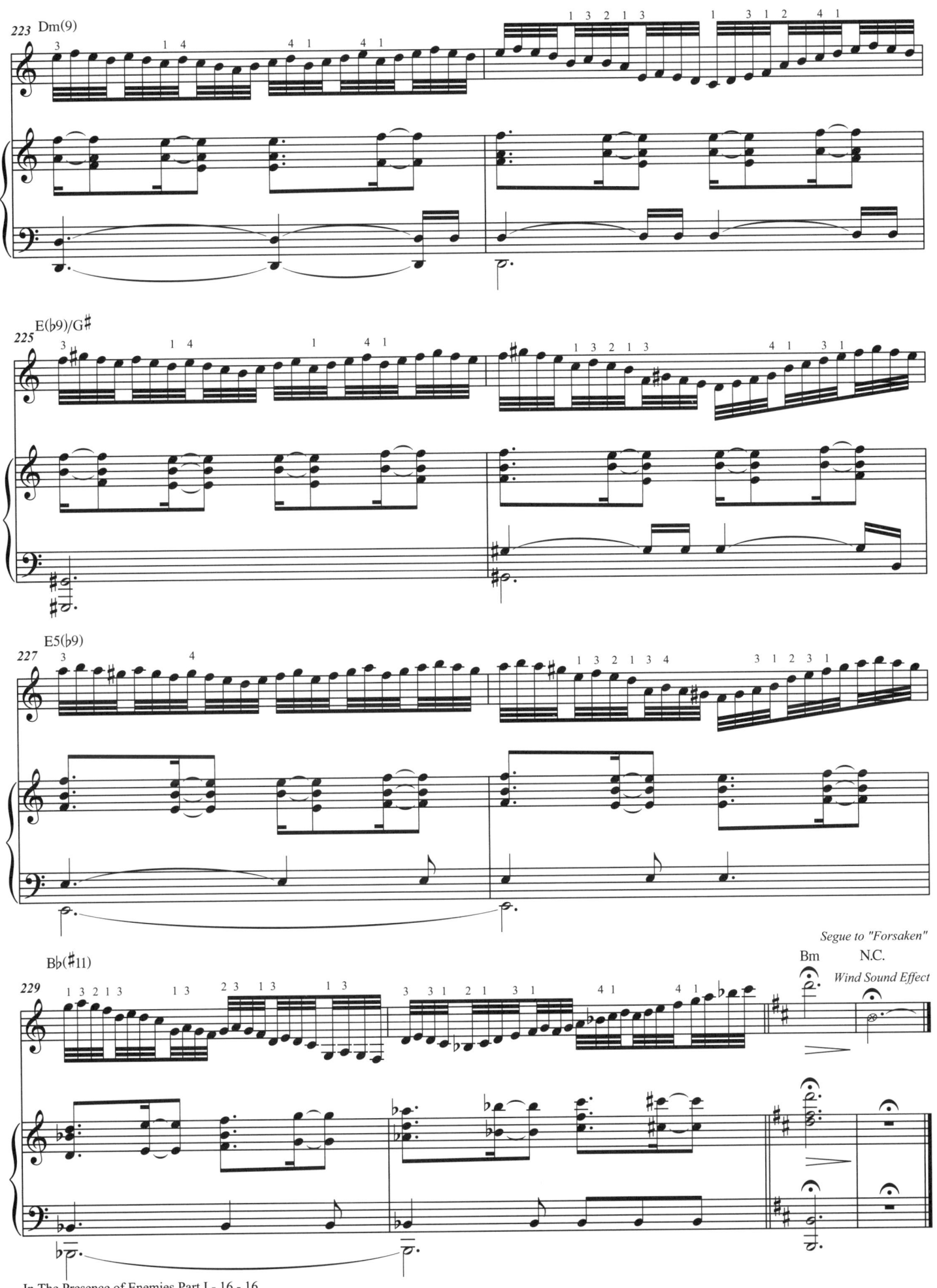

IN THE PRESENCE OF ENEMIES - PART II
The Heretic and The Dark Master
III. Heretic

Music by JAMES LABRIE, JOHN MYUNG,
JOHN PETRUCCI, MIKE PORTNOY, and JORDAN RUDESS
Lyrics by JOHN PETRUCCI

©2007 WB MUSIC CORP., YTSE JAMS, INC., WARNER-TAMERLANE PUBLISHING CORP., and KEY WIZ MUSIC
All Rights on behalf of Itself and YTSE JAMS, INC. administered by WB MUSIC CORP.
All Rights on behalf of Itself and KEY WIZ MUSIC administered by WARNER-TAMERLANE PUBLISHING CORP.
All Rights Reserved

IV. The Slaughter of The Damned

V. The Reckoning

"It's time for your reckoning."

VI. Salvation

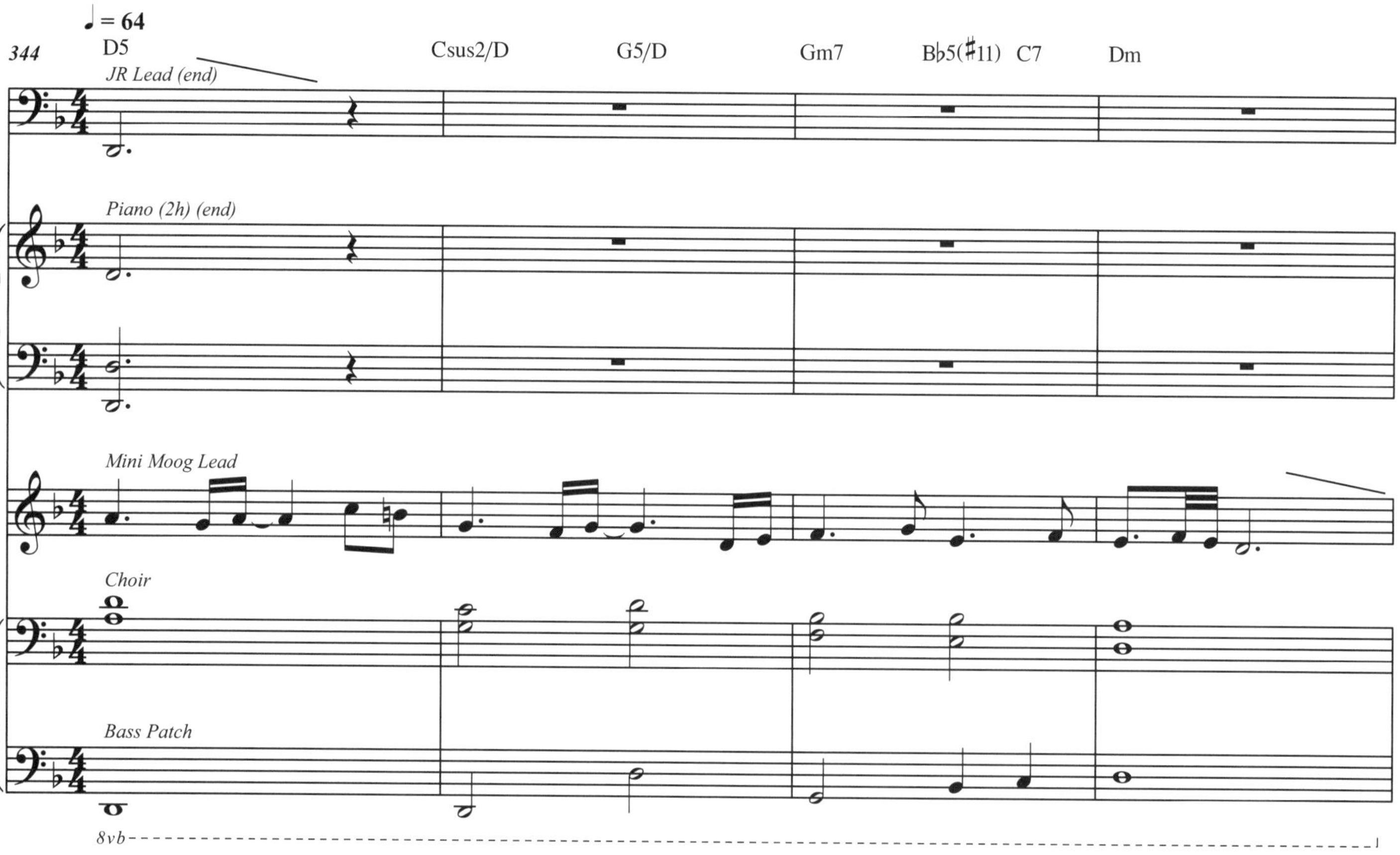

Polyphonic Lead Playing: The Lost Etude

You are gonna wish this one was lost by time you finish with it! It's not going away, so DEAL WITH IT!

The passage in "The Ministry of Lost Souls" that inspired this etude is a special point for me in every Dream Theater performance. I can always tell my level of preparedness by the way I pull this off. It combines quick playing of thirds and sixths as well as a technique I refer to as the "lazy pinky" technique, although there is not much "lazy" about it!

The "lazy pinky" idea started as a blues piano riff concept, and basically refers to the idea of letting the fifth finger of the right hand fall along with other lower notes while playing passages. The important goal here is to develop your skill for playing a combination of single notes and double notes within the moving line. Look out for some cool syncopation between the right hand and left hand at measure 6. I love bouncing rhythmically between the two hands.

The inspiration for this etude (page 190) is from measure 181 (page 203) of "The Ministry of Lost Souls" from *Systematic Chaos*.

Photo © Atsushi Sato

THE LOST ETUDE

By JORDAN RUDESS

© 2008 KEY WIZ MUSIC (BMI)
All Rights Reserved
Used by Permission

THE MINISTRY OF LOST SOULS

Music by JAMES LABRIE, JOHN MYUNG,
JOHN PETRUCCI, MIKE PORTNOY, and JORDAN RUDESS
Lyrics by JOHN PETRUCCI

©2007 WB MUSIC CORP., YTSE JAMS, INC., WARNER-TAMERLANE PUBLISHING CORP., and KEY WIZ MUSIC
All Rights on behalf of Itself and YTSE JAMS, INC. administered by WB MUSIC CORP.
All Rights on behalf of Itself and KEY WIZ MUSIC administered by WARNER-TAMERLANE PUBLISHING CORP.
All Rights Reserved

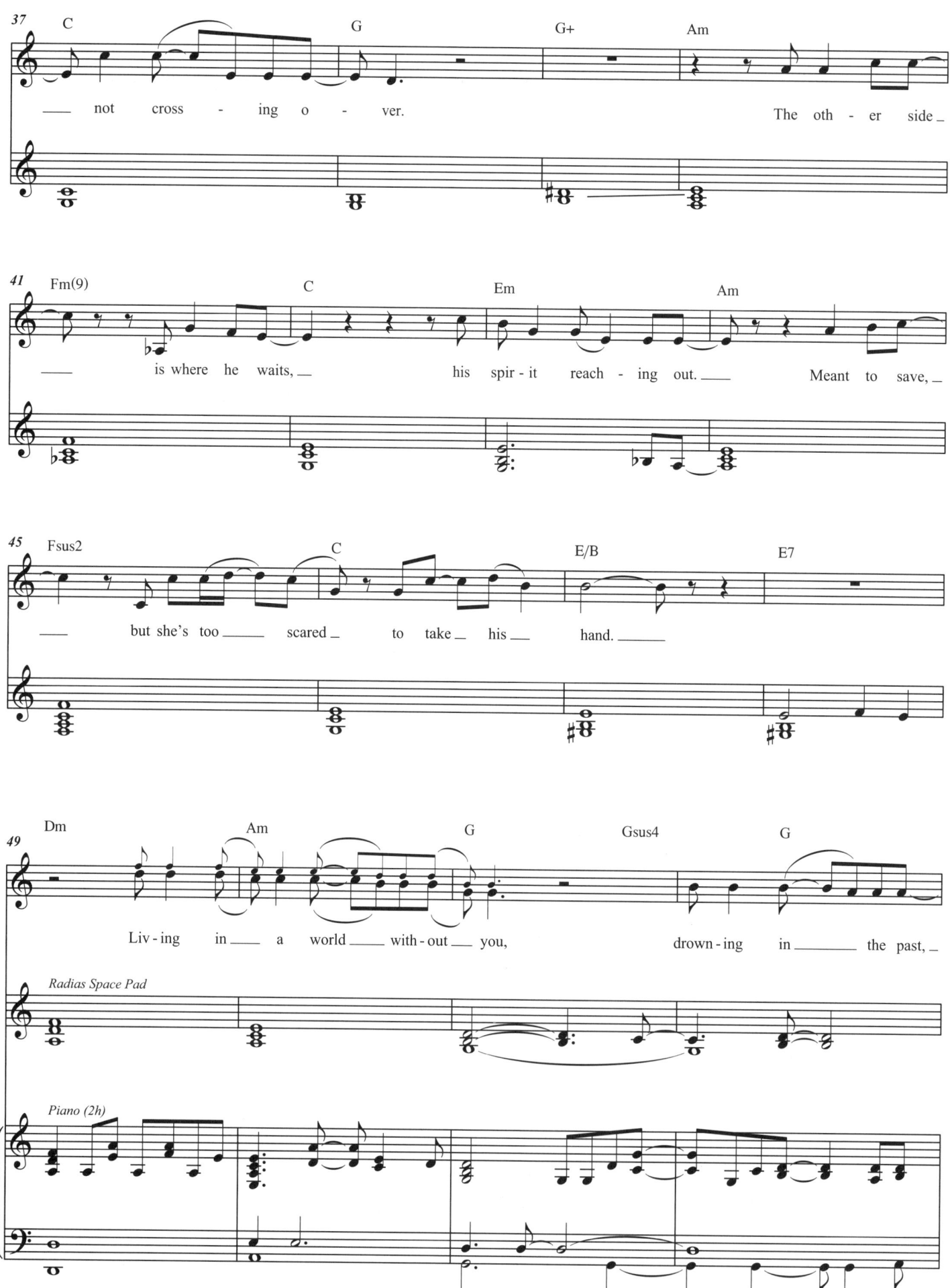